REVIVED BY JESUS CHRIST

HIS WRATH IS COMING

Manuel Giorgi

New Harbor Press
RAPID CITY, SD

Giorgi/New Harbor Press
1601 Mt. Rushmore Rd, Ste 3288
Rapid City, SD 57701
www.newharborpress.com

Ordering Information:
Quantity sales. Special discounts are available on quantity purchases by corporations, associations, and others. For details, contact the "Special Sales Department" at the address above.

Revived by Jesus Christ/Holmes. -- 1st ed.
ISBN 978-1-63357-443-4

The Truth About:
The Return of Jesus Christ
The Rapture
The End of the Age
The Love of God
The Catholic Church
AND
A Chilling Message
From Jesus Christ about the Second Coming
AND MUCH MORE

Exodus 32:10

10: "Now therefore let me alone, that my wrath may burn hot against them and I may consume them, in order that I may make a great nation of you."

John 11:42–44

42: "I knew that you always hear me, but I said this on account of the people standing around, that they may believe that you sent me."

43: When he had said these things, he cried out with a loud voice, "Lazarus, come out."

44: The man who had died came out, his hands and feet bound with linen strips, and his face wrapped with a cloth. Jesus said to them, "Unbind him, and let him go."

The Coming of the Son of Man
Luke 21:25

25: "And there will be signs in sun and moon and stars, and on the earth distress of nations in perplexity because of the roaring of the sea and the waves,

26: people fainting with fear and with foreboding of what is coming on the world. For the powers of the heavens will be shaken.

This is the true account of what happened to me. I died for 30–40 minutes on January 10, 2018. I spent that time with Jesus Christ. Over the last five years my relationship with Jesus Christ has gotten stronger and stronger. I have received numerous revelations, some dreams and visions. They were all from Jesus Christ. He has been helping me since that day to warn all. The day I got home all I could feel was the presence of the Father, Jesus Christ, and the Holy Spirit. I will go through what happened to me physically, emotionally, and spiritually. There are several important things Jesus wants people to know. This was not a "near-death experience." I was clinically dead for over half an hour; no pulse, not in a hospital, dead.

Jesus Christ told me that the world right now is the same as when God flooded the earth. We have taken God out of everything. The fear of the wrath of God is gone. Most people spend their time on different apps, such as Facebook, Twitter, Instagram, and many others. We have become lovers of ourselves. How many views can I get, flooding the Internet with pictures of us. God has simply allowed all of us to do what we want, because not many are spending any time with God. The last time that this happened God started over. He flooded the entire earth. He allowed Noah, his family, and animals to start over.

This time it will be different. Jesus Christ is coming with all his power and glory and showing the world that he is God. He will hand over all the followers that he saved by dying on the cross to his Father. Those are all the children of God. Then everyone else will be judged by God the Father. That day everyone will hear the roar of the oceans and feel the heavens shake for our Lord and Savior's glorious return. Every knee shall bend, and everyone's tongue will confess Jesus Christ as God. Some will be crying with happiness, because we have been praying for his return. The rest will be crying because they will already know their fate. God is not taking everyone to heaven. Nobody will have any more time. Nobody will be able to say they did not know. Everyone's salvation is between God and the person.

For the last 300 years, pastors, priests, and people made a lot of money telling us false information. I knew I had to explain this. Jesus Christ gave me the ability to interpret Bible verses correctly. He also gives me revelations about the more difficult verses that I did not initially understand. I completely explained the end of the age correctly with Bible verses that were right in front of us. The worst tribulations have already happened, according to Jesus, and there is no rapture. I also tell the truth about the Catholic Religion, Mormonism, Judaism, and Islam. I use the Word of God to correctly interpret the truth and easily dismiss the things that have been made up. Jesus spent a lot of time with me to tell everyone the truth. He kept giving me revelations, pointing me to verses, and letting me see the truth. A lot of my words in this book describe information that God gave to me about the meaning of those Bible verses. I use a lot of Bible verses that show that everything is from God. When I say that I have a revelation from God, it is something specific that God brings to my attention and explains it to me. I did a lot of praying and talking to God and made sure that everything I wrote down was true. That was why I needed time to be able to explain several chapters of this book. When I died, God gave me a lot of information and it has taken years for me to understand. I always keep Jesus Christ close because he is the one who gave me the information and he is the one who explains everything along with the Holy Spirit. Jesus Christ is the one who revived me and blessed me with the Holy Spirit. Nobody is saved if Jesus Christ is not God. That is why Jesus told me that he is the Way and the Truth and the Life. Nobody can be in the presence of the Father unless you go through Jesus Christ. I know he is God, and this is true. I had no heartbeat, no pulse, and no breathing machine for over 30 minutes. I will try to explain that time the best I can.

In December of 2022 I received a vision from Jesus. I told God I cannot finish this book without knowing everything that happened when I died. I told God I cannot move forward without that information. A week later Jesus Christ gave me a dream. Jesus was showing me that he has been teaching me for the past five years. A month later, I received a vision; Jesus said I was ready to know what he told me when I died. It all made sense and brought everything together. It was what happened during those 30 minutes that my body was dead. His message was about the information in this book. I would not have understood it if I remembered it when I was revived. His final message was an exciting and revealing look into the return of Jesus Christ. I was so surprised by what Jesus told me. It is also a warning. As you think of each word Jesus said to me, he mentions there are not many born-again Christians or people that know him. He also mentions the anger of the Father, with so many that does not fear his wrath. It is only getting worse. I go over this when I tell you what happened when I died.

Disclosure: The knowledge God gave me goes beyond what is taught in the Bible. It is knowledge of the war that is going on that nobody can see. Due to me getting this information when I was in my spirit form, along with Jesus Christ, I can see and feel certain things in the spiritual world. Satan is trying everything he can to keep our hearts away from God. There are things all around us. None of us can see it or hear it. It is a vicious war for souls. In the end, the book of life has everyone that is going to heaven. Please get close to Jesus Christ. He is our protector. He defeated everything so that in the end, it is our free will that will decide our relationship with God.

It is not my responsibility to make anyone believe the Words of God in this book. Only God can open your eyes to the actual Words of God. My words are useless.

John 8:45-47

45: But because I tell the truth, you do not believe me. 46: Which one of you convicts me of sin? If I tell the truth, why do you not believe me? 47: whoever is of God hears the words of God. The reason why you do not hear them is that you are not of God."

CONTENTS

CHAPTER 1

DYING

I grew up in the Catholic religion. Both of my parents were religious so that was all I knew. I went to catechism from kindergarten until I made my confirmation. We would go to church on and off. I completed all my sacraments. There were some things that bothered me about it, but not enough to switch religions. As I started getting older, I would still try to get to church, I would pray often, and I even prayed the rosary sometimes. I always had a good relationship with God, the Father, but not with Jesus or the Holy Spirit.

From when I was about twenty there were just things going on that I did not understand. I would read the Bible and I just was not getting it; it did not make sense to me. That was getting frustrating. Then things even got worse for me. Every single time I walked into a Catholic church, I would just get this lump in my throat. Once it started it never stopped. I have not gone into a Catholic church since I died. The last time I was in the Catholic church was when my father passed away, six months before my cardiac arrest. I had a good relationship with the Father, but hardly any with Jesus or the Holy Spirit. I was feeling uncomfortable going into a Catholic church and I did not understand the Bible. I got to the point where I did not want any part of the church, just God.

I did not have Jesus or the Holy Spirit in my life. I was not baptized with the Holy Spirit. I am beyond blessed. Jesus saved me and I do not know why. I do not deserve any of God's blessings, none of us do. We are all enemies to God until he saves us. Throughout all this, God the Father was drawing me in. The Father draws you in and then Jesus saves us. I did not know anything about how all that worked. Jesus saved me literally, my body and my soul. I was blessed with the Holy Spirit by Jesus while I was with him.

It's been five years, and everyone is different. The thing about when I died that is different from some is the amount of time that I was dead. I've read about what happens when you stop breathing and it is scary. Your brain starts to die within minutes without oxygen and it is normally completely dead after fifteen minutes. I obviously went beyond that, but even if it was only ten minutes, my brain would be mostly dead. It has taken me all this time to unravel, understand, and remember certain things that happened when I died. The three big things I remember are being in the presence of Jesus Christ, the knowledge I received, and the feeling of love and protection from Jesus Christ.

There are three reasons why I decided to write this book. I know there are things God wants explained that he is not happy about. I can literally feel how God feels about certain things. The other reason is to prove that God is constantly performing miracles every day. I am proof that God is making the impossible possible at any point he chooses. The last, and most important reason, for me writing this, is because Jesus told me to. The sad part is that a lot of people will dismiss this as a freak thing that happened or that it did not really happen. Trust me, I have all the medical records, along with the bills, to easily prove this happened. You can ask the first responders, the hospital, my doctors, staff, and my family. I have a sixteen-year-old son, and this was a traumatic experience that he went through.

I will use the Bible to further prove that the messages from God have been known for many, many years. I had so much knowledge from God that I could not process it. Finally, after five years, the gift of interpreting Bible verses started getting stronger. The information that Jesus gave me was all making sense. Now the ability to explain topics like a rapture event and the end of days was easy for me to see the truth. On top of that, I could feel how God feels about those topics. You do not have to believe me, I let the Bible explain everything.

How It Happened

Sometime in 2016 I started getting these episodes.
I would start getting a slight pain in the upper left part of my chest, right near my collarbone. After about forty-five seconds of light pain, I would get severe pain in the same spot for 2–3 minutes. Then it would just go away. I went to my cardiologist, and he did a full work-up. blood tests, ultrasound of my heart, stress test, and a specialized MRI test with contrast. This test is rarely done, but he did not want to do a cardiac catheterization because of the risk of complications. After all the tests were done my heart was fine. He did not see anything abnormal. So, he treated my high blood pressure. I was getting these episodes anywhere from once a week to once a month. I remember in December 2017 I was getting the episodes at the same time, normally from 8 a.m. to 12 p.m. I could not find anything different to what I was doing. At that point I stuck to the same exact diet. I found out I would get them less if I had the same diet. It was basically a high-protein diet. I was working out 4–5 days a week. Working out never caused an episode at that point. It turned out to be something that I just lived with and went on with my life,

In November 2017 I felt the Father pulling me towards him. I was feeling closer and closer. I was talking to God all the time. At the same time, I was starting to get revelations. There were some things I could not understand; then, out of nowhere, I would get the answer. In late December I was having an episode and I was praying to God to not let something happen to me at work. I am quiet and kept to myself. I hate drama. Work is the last place I wanted to die. Plus, it could take an hour before anyone found me early in the morning.

On Wednesday, January 10th, 2018, I woke up as I do every day. I was off from work that day and I had some errands to run. I headed to the bathroom to get cleaned up a bit. It was around 9 in the morning. My mother heard a loud bang, and it was me hitting the floor. She opened the door, and she heard the "agonal gasps."So, she heard my last breath. She then started yelling my name and moving me to see if I would wake up. At that point I was dead. That's all it took. It literally happened in seconds. She called 911. The fire station at that time was maybe two blocks away. They got there within ten minutes. My mother also called my brothers and they got to the house maybe ten minutes later. From my medical records, I did not have a heartbeat for at least thirty minutes. They tried everything they could, they even used Narcan, thinking I overdosed on something. At some point they hooked up the LUCAS machine to do the chest compressions. I have a permanent mark on my chest from it. It was God's will that they kept going for half an hour. They could have stopped after 10–15 minutes. After 30–35 minutes they got a faint pulse, and they took me to Fatima Hospital. You might be wondering why they tried for so long. They normally stop after 20–25 minutes. My uncle is a dispatcher for the North Providence Fire Department. He heard the call come through and went to my house. That is why they kept going. God thinks of everything.

I was shocked at least three times at my house. Three more times at Fatima Hospital. I was in the emergency room, and I had another episode of "ventricular fibrillation."My heart was beating so erratically it was not doing anything. So, I was shocked again. From the time I died to the time they got my heart beating normally and me on a respirator was at least 40–60 minutes. I was shocked six times. Regardless of how long, they did not expect me to have a fully functioning brain and I was still in bad shape. Once I was stable, the tests showed my heart ejection fraction was 30–35 percent, my kidneys and liver were failing. The breathing machine was keeping me alive. They told my family that night that they were not expecting me to make it through the night. The one thing they did not consider is God.

What Happened Spiritually

When I got home from the hospital, I could feel God's love. The presence of the Father, Jesus Christ, and the Holy Spirit surrounded me as I tried to make sense of what happened. The love I felt was not like anything I felt before. The presence of God was all around me. At times I felt like I was floating. I was in the hospital for thirteen days. I only remember the last couple of days, so when I got home everything that I went through hit me all at once. The feelings were so strong, but I knew that, in time, all the feelings would go away. I had a lot of emotions going through my head and it was almost overwhelming. I now had all new information about God that I did not have before. I was struggling with why I came back, what the purpose was. I still had no idea what caused the cardiac arrest, so I was worried about it happening again. I was worried about getting shocked by the ICD (implanted cardioverter-defibrillator) in my chest. Before I left the hospital, because they did not know the cause, they had to put it in so that I would have some protection. God just kept telling me to read the Bible, find whatever I can about him so the knowledge will make more sense. The love of God gave me the strength to just relax and give everything some time. I had this overwhelming thirst for information about God.

I initially did not remember everything that I saw after I died. Several months after I got home, I started having dreams about it.

When I woke up, I would write it down. As I wrote it down the more questions I had. I get revelations from God about certain things. He will give me something to focus on, reveal to me what certain things mean and how he feels about certain things. There are things I saw, but I could not remember them 100 percent. I really got multiple revelations about that night, just not everything that happened. God's response is always the same, his Word is everything, so do not worry about what you see. I can say that your mind never stops. As soon as your body dies, you leave it. After my heart stopped, my spirit rose. I did see a bright light. My eyes adjusted and I was at a door. All I could feel was the presence of God. I knew Jesus Christ was inside the structure ahead of me.

I could feel how it is when you are a spirit, the knowledge and love you feel. I am going to go over all of that. I had a vision in December of 2022. Jesus told me everything that happened when I died; it made sense because finally all my questions were answered. There are parts that are chilling. I just needed to know and finally found out everything and it completely agrees with this book. Before I tell you about all of that, I need to tell you the other side of it. If I was not saved, I would have gone straight to hell.

Hell

There is another side to all of this, and we all need to think about it. The love of God is so strong, and it is all you will ever need. I cannot imagine living without the love and protection of God. The only place where you cannot feel God is hell. This is a big topic that I must explain. You get the torture, agony, despair, and you just want to die because of Satan and his angels. Plus, you do not feel the presence of God at all. It truly is sad to see just one soul go to hell. The knowledge God gave me has vivid descriptions of hell. Right now, hell is located at the center of the earth. When the second death occurs, hell will be a lake of fire and there is a bottomless pit just for Satan. There are millions of people in hell. You will remember everything. You will also remember every time God sent one of his servants on earth to try and teach you more about God. You remember your family and the things you could have done differently. According to Mary K. Baxter (*A Divine Revelation of Hell*), the souls in hell constantly burn. They feel the pain, some have worms all inside them, the smell is sickening, demons constantly torture them. You can hear the screams and moans of other souls, but you cannot talk to anyone. It is beyond your worst nightmare. Jesus pleads with all of us to repent and believe in him!

Matthew 13:41–42

41: The Son of Man will send his angels, and they will gather out of his kingdom all causes of sin and all law-breakers,
42: and throw them into the fiery furnace. In that place there will be weeping and gnashing of teeth.

Once there, you will never feel God again. You know that you can never leave. The darkness alone consumes you. There will be intense heat, torture, loneliness, thirst, and hunger. You will pray for death. The demons love to torture you because you are in the image of God, and they hate God. The demons are very strong and absolutely hate anyone in the image of God. The sad thing is that Jesus defeated all of this for all of us. If you do not truly love and believe in Jesus Christ, hell is your only option. Salvation is between God and yourself. Everything such as rats, spiders, and snakes are there, but they are enormous in size and strength. Satan loves to lie and torment souls. Whatever you fear the most will be there with you forever. You could be locked up in a cage and have demons inside just torturing you. People that always say, "I'm going to hell anyway," should realize how bad it will be. Just remember that God created all things. All the beautiful things that we have on this earth were made by God. How bad of a place would you think he made for Satan? Our minds cannot comprehend what we are all facing, good or bad. When we die it will be unexplainable, just as his love really is. With a love so strong from God, you have to think about the opposite. God hates sin. All of the strong feelings of love, God has the same hatred for evil and sin.

2 Thessalonians 1:8–9

8: in flaming fire, inflicting vengeance on those who do not know God and on those who do not obey the gospel of our Lord Jesus.
9: They will suffer the punishment of eternal destruction, away from the presence of the Lord and from the glory of his might

I had several revelations about hell. The knowledge God gave me has a lot about hell. Things you do not think of like the smell and despair. You think about your family. It is physically, mentally, and spiritually torturing, It was meant for Satan and the fallen angels, but that is where God sends the unsaved souls. I thought about hell for two weeks. I read everything about it and pulled the knowledge that I have about it from my head. I cried every day and kept praying to God, thanking him for saving me. I was sick to my stomach just thinking about flesh being burnt off and wanting a drop of water. You must pray for those that are lost. Do your best every day, keep God always close to you because death can come at any second and will come to all of us. I feel the presence of God every day. I do not take that for granted. It motivates me to do more and more to help others to know Jesus. Bill Wiese's *23 Minutes in Hell* is another excellent book. Please read it. His explanation of hell is 100 percent true also. My knowledge from Jesus verifies that explanation of hell. Everything I read or watched about God after I died becomes real to me, if it is true.

Matthew 10:28

28: And do not fear those who kill the body but cannot kill the soul. Rather fear him who can destroy both soul and body in hell.

When I thought about hell, I kept writing things down. These are just some of the things I wrote down way before I wrote any books:

Once there, there is no more God. You cannot feel him anymore. There is no hope. You know that you can never leave this place. There is absolutely no love there and everything about Jesus is absent. except what is in your mind. The darkness alone consumes you. You are filled with hopelessness, fear, and agony, in pain forever, in intense heat. There are no liquids, no light, nobody to talk to, and nobody cares. The maggots will constantly eat your flesh, you will feel every bite. The only thing that you will seek is death, but it will never come. The fire will burn your flesh down to the bone, but the worms still remain. Then the fire dies down, your flesh fills you again only to be melted and completely burnt again. You remember your family, your loved ones, the things that you did here on earth and it is all magnified. You will also remember every time that someone brought up Jesus, God, or anything else that could have led you to salvation.

There are things I did not include. There are things that happen that are not appropriate for this book. If you think about the most torturous things, multiply them by infinity, and then you can really picture what is happening in hell. Just think about the fact that we are only here for eighty or ninety years. These things happen for eternity. There is nowhere in the Bible that has any time limit in hell. It says for eternity. God never changes. Just let that sink in. I pray that you find Jesus. He took all this torture so that God's children do not have to. You must find him!

Matthew 25:41

41: "Then he will say to those on his left, 'Depart from me, you cursed, into the eternal fire prepared for the devil and his angels.

Revelation 20:15

15: And if anyone's name was not found written in the book of life, he was thrown into the lake of fire.

Lately, it seems that I find more and more people that do not care about God or religion. Too many people are choosing the world. I think some of that has to do with TV, the Catholic Church, and the removal of God from everything. Hell is real. It is constant torture, you remember everything, and you want to die but you can't, and you will be there for eternity. Seventy to eighty years is a blink of an eye compared to eternity. I also do not believe that life right now can continue in the same direction. It is getting to the point where you can almost compare it to when God flooded the earth. This is not the time to get into all of that. I just cannot tell you how powerful God's love really is, then, not think about all those people that will never feel it. I can also say this on behalf of Jesus Christ, it hurts him for every soul that goes to hell because he provided the only way to avoid it.

Satan knows that he turned this world into an immediate gratification world. People want everything now. You want an immediate benefit instead of a longer future benefit. This generation needs everything right now. People get aggravated if they must wait for something for a few days or a week. Why have so many things become same-day delivery? There are hundreds of apps and games on your phone that give you immediate gratification. When was the last time you prayed and prayed for something, and it took six months to get it? You were so grateful to get it. It was worth all that time. It takes a long time to read the Bible. It can take years for spiritual goals. Satan has everyone in the "right now" generation. That is not how real life works. Get away from your phone, computer, and TV. Light a candle, read the Bible, talk to God. Tell him how you feel, tell him what your long-term goals are. That is what will change your life. We must be different. We cannot follow what the world does. Your immediate gratification can turn into an eternity in hell.

Luke 16:22–25

22: The poor man died and was carried by the angels to Abraham's side. The rich man also died and was buried,
23: and in Hades, being in torment, he lifted up his eyes and saw Abraham far off with Lazarus at his side.
24: And he called out, 'Father Abraham, have mercy on me, and send Lazarus to dip the end of his finger in water and cool my tongue, for I am in anguish in this flame.'
25: But Abraham said, 'Child, remember that you in your lifetime received your good things, and Lazarus in like manner bad things; but now he is comforted here, and you are in anguish.

This was before Jesus was crucified. In the center of the earth there is Hades, which is hell, and they had another side for all the people that were going to heaven, but they had to wait until Jesus ascended into heaven before they could all go there. I put this verse in just so you could see how bad hell really is. The person that was in hell, all he wanted was just a drop of water. That is just one small verse that gives you a very small look into Hades.

I accept that God created certain people for his purposes that he knew they would ultimately go to hell. There is no excuse today with all the information available, and the number of people reaching out, that people cannot find information about God. The problem is free will. People just do not want to live life hating the world. They love it too much. There are a lot of people that say there is no God or that God is going to bring everyone to heaven. Other people like to use science to explain everything. These people are listening to Satan. Did my brain go without oxygen that long and nothing happened to it? How can science explain that? There are numerous miracles that God does every day. I'm here as an eyewitness. Jesus Christ is real, loving, holy, and powerful. You cannot dream when your heart stops. Your soul lives forever and goes to one of two places, heaven or hell. The choice is yours. The way I view it is that salvation is between you and God. We cannot figure out why one person goes to hell and the other doesn't. Whomever God reaches out to save and do his will is completely between God and that person. I never will question it; it is not my business, and I will never be able to comprehend God's knowledge or why things happen the way they do. I just trust God 100 percent and question nothing. Please find Jesus Christ. I am pleading with you. Once you die, it's too late if you have not found him. God does these things to warn you. He gives some people visions, he appears to certain people, he tries in many ways to warn you that none of this is a joke. A bunch of us are blessed to be able to tell our story. It is not for us; it is for you. I find myself watching a lot of murder documentaries. When they talk to the one that just killed a bunch of people or their spouses, I have noticed something. Most of them have no remorse.

Genesis 6:5–6

5: The LORD saw that the wickedness of man was great in the earth, and that every intention of the thoughts of his heart was only evil continually.
6: And the LORD regretted that he had made man on the earth, and it grieved him to his heart.

This shows you how God feels when all he sees is evil. God had said this before the Flood. Thankfully Noah was righteous and walked with the Lord. Without Noah, God was ready to blot all of man out. It grieved his heart because of the love God has for us. The problem is that man has evil tendencies and the only way that we can get rid of all of that is through Jesus Christ. What many people do not realize is that God had already wiped off all of man once, with the exception of Noah and his family. Hell is real, God never changes, the path to the Father is very narrow. Most people think that God is just going to take everybody to heaven after they die. That is very far from the truth and the only way for all these people to know the truth is keep putting the Word of God out there.

If you get up and walk away right now and you are not saved, it could be too late. If Jesus has not saved you, you could stand up and fall to the floor and have a cardiac arrest just as I did. It took a split second, and I was dead. We are running out of time. I am not a prophet, so I do not know when the second coming of Jesus is. As I look around where I live, what's going on in the country, and what's going on around the world, I really do not know how much longer God is going to hold off. Sometimes I see people doing good things, then I think to myself maybe it's not that bad; but, then, if I ever watch the news, I can see how far evil has spread. It is in our schools, it is in our neighborhoods, it is in our towns, cities, our nation, and even worse in places around the world. There is one verse that the second coming of Christ is close. I will go over it later, but Jesus says, "It will be like in the time of Noah." Everybody is just living their regular lives and then it just happens. There will be no warning.

Jesus

I would pray daily to be able to fully remember that time. This went on for years. With all the revelations and dreams, the majority of what happened when I died was blocked. There was a veil over it. After going through intense praying, not giving up on the book, there was a reason why it was not revealed to me.

On November 10, 2022, I had a dream from Jesus Christ. I was in a maze. I was running through it, then I would look up and Jesus Christ would point which way to go. Then I would go further and get to an intersection, I looked up and Jesus pointed which way to go. This went on for a while. It was vivid, I really saw Jesus Christ. After the dream, things started to feel different. Jesus was telling me that he has been guiding me. I was reaching a point that I've been trying to reach since the cardiac arrest, to be one with God. It brought back feelings of when I was with Jesus. Overall, it brought my faith up to another level.

On December 7, 2022, a month away from year five since my cardiac arrest, Jesus gave me a vision that is the main point of the message he wants everyone to know. I remember I just finished at the gym, I was at the drive-through to get coffee, still praying to God about it. I got a flood of information from Jesus Christ. I am thinking about it as his words just kept going. As I was getting this information, I was getting visions along with the revelations. When I died, my spirit went to be with Jesus. Every time I thought about being in heaven with Jesus, it was always dark, and I did not know why. As soon as I got home, I immediately wrote down everything that Jesus was telling me. I remember it now. I knew what it was about, there was just one thing I had in the conversation that I never thought of. That was one of the reasons why God hid it from my memory for almost five years. The main thing that was blocked is huge. So, I will tell you exactly what happened.

My body collapsed and my soul immediately was in a tunnel, I was flying through it. I went to a fork and could go left or right. My spirit went to the right, I slowed down, frame by frame, I saw going left would take me to hell. When I stopped, I went to be with Jesus

Christ. I was outside a room at a door. I could see that it was filled with books. It was very dark outside, but Jesus said, "Come in." Jesus was in the middle of the room. He was sitting at a desk reading a gold book. I could see his hair just glistening on his robe. I knew that Jesus knew every word in every book in the room. I felt Jesus pulling me towards him. I was about two feet away and I just dropped to my knees. I felt his love for me. I will never be able to explain it. I was home and I felt fulfilled. Jesus said to me, "I am the Way, the Truth, and the Life. I am going to give you information that will help you get these messages to everyone." He turned towards me and put his hand on my forehead. I felt a rush of things enter my mind and the Holy Spirit entering me. I just kneeled there, just feeling relaxed and loved. Jesus got up and walked out and he said, "Come with me."

It was a beach, and it was dark, then got very bright and Jesus started speaking to me. He is taller than me. We were both in spirit form. I am five feet seven inches, Jesus looked about six feet. His face was perfect, beautiful, and unique. He resembled all men, a combination of races, but was his own, not like anyone else. He was wearing a beautiful robe. It was mostly blue but was multicolored near the top. It was by far the best color blue I have ever seen. It was dark blue. The multicolor area was in his upper chest, and it was glistening and bright. All colors could be seen. The love and protection I felt is unexplainable. My feelings, senses, and knowledge were unbelievably heightened. I knew I was in the presence of God. It was embedded in my mind that the Father, Son, and Holy Spirit are One God with three different persons. It is not like here, where you can argue in your mind about it. I was walking next to him, and my mind just knew that this was OK. Just as when I kneeled next to him, I just knew to kneel. I knew in my mind that I knew a lot more about God and creation, but I could only focus on Jesus Christ and every word he spoke. I was unable to speak because I was overwhelmed with information that I never knew before. This is everything that he told me, word for word.

"Welcome, my brother, my servant, Manuel. I really like your name, that is why I gave it to you a long time ago. I love you and I have things to tell you. I had prepared the way for everyone to be saved. The problem is free will. There was the Fall of Adam, the Flood with Noah, the teachings of Abraham, then Moses; the final event was after my crucifixion, the Holy Spirit was released into the whole world. You were interested in God from a young age. You just did not get the correct information. Our Father draws those that are seeking him. As you got older our Father drew you in closer and closer, then it was time for me to save you. There are several things that people need to know. After I ascended to heaven to be at the right hand of my Father, I became the High Priest for everyone on earth. Now, there are too many that do not want any part of the Father. They no longer fear his wrath and I will no longer hold my Father's hand back. The Father is angry, that is why you see darkness. Now the table has been set. Once all the guests arrive, then I will arrive. The Father knows when that is, and there are so many people that do not care. It is not a surprise. It is just upsetting. Just as I was upset in the garden before my crucifixion. I know it's going to happen, but it still hurts. This time was known before anything was created.

"I am the Way and the Truth and the Life. You will not know all of this until almost five years from now. I will be giving you information to stress the importance of this. You have been through a lot, and now you know we went through a lot together. I had to refine you enough to deliver this message. Nobody will ever get a date when I come again. This ungodliness on earth will not last forever. Now that this is being shown to you, everything will be in place. You have been waiting a long time for this. I will always be with you, as will the Holy Spirit and our Father. Your road will be worth it in the end. You knew of this day, in your mind, many years ago. You are blessed. Tell everyone, tell them of my messages. There is still time, but too much is lost now. We have known this, but this was the only way to find the true believers, the true children of God. People will have visions, but the only one I am telling is you. By the time you get this vision, you will have everything you need to complete the book. I will have already shown you the truth about everything chosen to be written in your book. People must not waste time. The main thing to be focused on is me. I can save all of them. I judge someone by what is in their heart. I gave you all the information, you can see what is happening around everyone. I had to open your eyes to see all that the enemy is currently doing. That is only for you. You need to see so this message will be urgent. You will keep telling these messages. I have known you for a long time. I planned this from the beginning of the world. I had to make you strong enough to tell people, with confidence, that we have arrived at a point where true born-again Christians are a very small percentage of the people in the world. Every generation that goes by knows less and less about God. Father has always hoped that people would be able to live with love in their hearts. When Cain killed Abel, it was a warning that original sin would be overcome by few. That is why it takes only but one sin to burn in hell for eternity. That one sin opens your eyes to good and evil. But I provide the only way. So much evil, if they could spend five minutes in hell, they would never sin again. The problem with that is the human mind cannot process it. The physical body would immediately die if it were exposed to hell for seconds. The Father breathes the air in man's lungs to produce life. His breath is so powerful, it cannot be killed. Yes, the body, but not the soul. It is time for you to finish the message. We do not calculate time here, but on earth; it is running out of it. These messages will be available to all. It is always up and down for you. That is how it must be for my servants. In dark times, remember, you are blessed. Not many do I allow to be with me before judgment. You reached a point where you feel me inside you all the time. It took a lot of challenges, but I am always with you. It is a little difficult because you are seeing this almost five years from now. Do not worry about who believes you and who does not, that is for the Father and I, as you know. Your blessings and happiness are coming. All you must do is point to me. Things will happen shortly after the book is published. There are many that I want to read all these words. The last thing I want to tell you is by the time this is revealed to you, the Father's time of anger will be over. For the past five years, the Father had been preparing his judgment for all. During this time, the Father was seeing all the sins of man. The Great White Judgment is near, the final judgment of all sinners. The lake of fire has been prepared for them. Those saved, the Father see's their sins no more. The time to act is coming. We are always with you, so be confident. Talk about us with confidence. For I chose you for a reason. It will be beautiful when I return. As I told you, no date will be given. Do not believe those that give an actual date, for I have not told anyone. Even though you know more about that time, do not tell anyone, unless I tell you to. You must go back. Time is important. The table is set. Guests are on their way. I Bless you in the name of our Father, the Holy Spirit, and I, your King, your brother, I AM. We are with you always. We have now reached the point that you and I are one. There is nothing that you will not do for me. Rest in me for a time. Your time is still to come. There will be more before I return. My servants will contact you soon. I will be showing the world my power and proving to all that I AM GOD! Never forget, I am your King, you are my servant, but you are also my brother. I take care of my family. Our Father takes care of all his children. Always trust me. Now, this message is finished. You will hear the roar of the water and feel the heavens shake. Then, you will be with me and all the Father's children." After this I went back to my body.

The Table Is Set

Revived by Jesus Christ

Daniel 2:20–23

20: Daniel answered and said: "Blessed be the name of God forever and ever, to whom belong wisdom and might.

21: He changes times and seasons; he removes kings and sets up kings; he gives wisdom to the wise and knowledge to those who have understanding;

22: he reveals deep and hidden things; he knows what is in the darkness, and the light dwells with him.

23: To you, O God of my fathers, I give thanks and praise, for you have given me wisdom and might, and have now made known to me what we asked of you, for you have made known to us the king's matter."

God, sometimes, will bring us to a level that provides us wisdom and reveals certain things to those that he chooses. This is a vision that Jesus shared with me for a reason. I know he is talking about the Second Coming. This is important information. I look at those words, I can feel how God feels about this. The Father is not happy with the way the world is trending. A lot of people do not realize it because they are not one with God. Others are blinded and feel like God is just taking his people off the earth. They do not see the big picture. It is judgment time for everyone. People will not get a second chance. There is no more time for people to see that God took all his people and Jesus is coming at some later time. Everyone has been given enough time and warnings to know. It angers God when people lead others to a false way because they misinterpret the Bible. We should not be telling people that they will be given a second chance. If you're telling people there will be a "rapture," then you are telling people to not worry about it, you can turn to Jesus after the Rapture, you will have more time.

This was the one thing I did not know about. The actual timing of the Second Coming. That this is the last prophecy left that Jesus

Christ gave us. "The table is set' was said twice, that was the first thing I noticed. Then Jesus tells me that, as of right now, the Father's anger is now over. I would think this table would have the elders of the Bible. Moses, Abraham, Noah, Elijah, and many other important people. All I know is I would love to talk to everyone at that table. The table is just symbolic obviously, but it is interesting to think about. Everything Jesus told me matches up exactly with the things I already mentioned. This is from five years ago, so how far along is it now? That's why this was a chilling revelation. For this one I needed something to back it up and know that was the final revelation for this book. Jesus did something to confirm this message is true. Hopefully now God will get this book out, so people will know that we do not have a lot of time. I was not expecting this at all. I thought we were going to have a lot of time. I am very happy that I finally know everything that happened when I died. I just was not expecting this. It upset me for a few days. So many people do not know, or care, what is coming. I cannot wait, but that is selfish. To become one with God is very difficult. But once you get there, you feel God running through your veins. He is all you think about. You realize you are the light in a dark world, and you fear nothing but God. I see a war going on now. Soon, it will reach the physical realm. But that is not what this book is about.

Jesus is amazing. When I died it created this relationship that grows every day. It almost feels like a portal that keeps Jesus and me always in contact with each other. I know that Jesus is omnipresent and is with everyone. Jesus reminded me that this exact situation was prophesied many years ago. . . The next thing I remember I was getting surgery the next morning for the ICD. That was my thirteenth day in the hospital. I woke up after three days, but I do not remember anything from those days. I died on January 10, 2018, and went home on January 23, 2018.

I cannot wait until I can sit down with Jesus and talk to him again. I have so many questions for him. I know that someday that will happen. I was blessed with everything that happened. I am also blessed with revelations frequently. I occasionally have dreams with Jesus in them. The dreams feel powerful. Every detail means something. The dreams feel the same as being a spirit. You just know that God is the Father, the Son, and the Holy Spirit. It is embedded in your mind. You have more information about creation, and you have a lot of answers to the questions you've always had. I did not feel any weight.

The biggest thing about this whole experience was as soon as I got home. I could feel the presence, love, protection, and realized that Jesus made all of this happen. I felt the Father, the Holy Spirit, and Jesus Christ and it was very strong. Absolutely everything looked and felt different. I could feel all the sin around me. I had stronger feelings about things than I ever had before. Everything in my room that had to do with the Catholic Church felt very disturbing. I had rosary beads hanging up, a picture of Mary and I believe a statue. They literally made me feel sick to my stomach. I had to remove them right away. I was a different creature. Everything outside looked different to me. I literally felt like I was in a foreign world. This was not my home. I could see and feel things were wrong and did not know why. Ultimately, Jesus Christ told me to take time and learn more, read the Bible.

I always felt different from everyone else. I was always isolating myself because I just wanted to be alone. I find myself still doing it sometimes, but I know I must be out there to be ready if someone needs to talk to me. Jesus really cares about all of us. He loves everyone. It's a love that no person can comprehend or describe. To be the creator of billions of people, love and know each one, I just cannot comprehend how God can do all of this. But he does. The Word of God and the knowledge of God is more powerful than anything else, except God himself. Whatever God wants me to do, I will do it without hesitation.

What I saw, how I felt in everything just came together. I did not know how I got the knowledge about God. I knew I had a cardiac arrest, and I could feel Jesus Christ all around me. I also did not know what happened when I died, but I knew I was in the presence of Jesus Christ. That was and is an amazing feeling. It wasn't a dream. I remember it and was able to figure out why I did not want to come back; with the love and protection, I felt home. I felt that God would tell me everything when the time was right. Now was the right time. I got the revelation that I was going to write a book in May of 2020, when they finally diagnosed me. Then, it was around February of 2021 that I knew I had to get going with it. It is unbelievable to me that every day I get closer and love God more and more. I feel the closest to God here on earth and when I first got home from the hospital, while reading the Bible, and when I write about him. But nothing compares to feeling God's love. I try to pray every day that eventually these words might reach one person and it will be the seed that the Father is planting. My words mean nothing. That is why I am using a lot of Bible verses, because those words ARE the true words of God and are very powerful. God uses us in many ways. He gave everyone different gifts. He puts things in our hearts to do. We may not understand it at that time, but it is all for the same reason, the glory of God. What I know in my soul is that it all happened for a reason. The knowledge and my relationship with the Father, Jesus Christ, and the Holy Spirit are all that matters.

There have been things I have read since I got back, and it felt so real to me as I read it. I read different books about people who had visions, dreams, or died and came back. Some of the things I can see and feel as if I was there. I am constantly getting revelations from God about things he wants me to do or explain something I do not understand. I always stay close to God. God has truly blessed me in ways I never thought of. There are still more things God wants me to do. I will figure all that out when the time is right for God.

If you ask me what it was like to be with Jesus, there are no words that I can use to describe it. Now, he is always here with me to love, protect, and guide me.

Blessings Start Right Away

Jesus gave me a revelation about how I have been blessed since that day, and it started a little before. Since the day I died I have the Holy Spirit, Jesus Christ, and the Father with me all the time. The Father was really drawing me in more and more as that day got closer. I was talking to him all the time; I was starting to understand different things. When I started at Lowe's I was just a seasonal employee. At that time, they would hire about thirty people and get rid of them after the busy season ended. When I work, I work hard. They offered me a part-time position and I was going to fill hours in two different departments. Then, I was offered a full-time position as a customer service associate. Then I moved up to a department sales associate. Then I died. I was out for three months, and they held my position. From there I tried to get the sales floor supervisor position. The second time I applied for it, I got that position. That was as far as I wanted to go, because I was writing my first book. Shortly before that, I was out again. That was when they finally found out the cause of my problem. From there, I wrote the first book, *I Died to Meet Jesus*. During that time when I started, the store was making about $23 million a year. Now, it has grown to an over $40 million dollar store. Then COVID started. We were essential, so we never closed. The store just kept growing. Then I got anemia and tore the tendon in my shoulder. I needed surgery, so I was out for three months again.

As I look back, I learned a lot of things while working there. How to lead people, I always hated talking in front of people, but now I do it all the time. I learned to be sensitive to other people's points of view. I became a good leader because I treat everyone with respect, I think of things from their perspective, and I allow them to come to me with any problem. So, I feel like I needed all those things to move forward. God put me in that situation to learn. I can say that I am a different person, with everything that happened over the last seven years. Now I feel as though I have learned everything I can from there. It is time for me to move on and take the next step. That step involves this book, being in front of people, telling them what God needs them to hear. It is all in God's hands. I do believe I am ready for the next step, but that is in God's hands.

The Gifts and Information God Gave Me

The information God gave me is all from the Bible. I just get a very strong feeling about it, and I know it is from God. I will give you an example. When I first got home, I knew the Catholic religion was false because things were added, the massive idolatry, purgatory, and sins being forgiven due to the Mass and the Eucharist. The presence of a statue of Mary, the mother of Jesus Christ, was making me feel a way that I never felt before. It was not because of who it was, it was because it was a statue of worship. It was not a statue of Jesus Christ. I immediately knew I had to get it out of my personal space. There were some pictures and rosary beads hanging up. I had to take everything down. From their presence I was getting feelings of disgust. It took years to get the information from the Bible. For two years I would write down information and then find the Bible verses.

Then, while I would read Bible verses, I could interpret them and sometimes feel how God feels about it. An example is "before Abraham was, I Am." I know there are verses about that in the Old Testament and I could feel that they are strong verses. Jesus was telling everyone, "I am God." So, it is very important that people understand that

Jesus is God. Jesus also said it to me. All his love and words radiated right through me.

Those two things were gifts given to me by Jesus Christ. That is why I can read the Bible and understand what God is talking about. Sometimes, I must go back and make sure I explain what they mean; some are difficult to understand. Sometimes I can read a verse and know the meaning but cannot find the supporting verses. Those take time and prayers. Plus, God is God; he does not have to give me any answers. For the verses, I cannot interpret every verse. If I need to know what a verse means and I cannot interpret it, I tell God and pray and in time he reveals it to me.

CHAPTER 2

THE PHYSICAL BATTLE

Even though I died and came back, the battle was not over. The doctors still did not know what caused the cardiac arrest. For four years, I was getting these 3–5-minute episodes where I would get chest pains (sometimes severe) and my heart would beat erratically. It started two years before the cardiac arrest. My cardiologist did a full workup but could not find anything. At that time, it would only happen a couple times a month. I just learned to live with it. Working out never caused it. When it did happen, it was in the morning. I just lived with it. I still did not realize that these episodes are what caused the cardiac arrest. After the cardiac arrest I did not get any of those episodes for a few months. I've been working out for ten years and I just wanted to get back to the gym.

I could not wait to get to the gym. I lost fifteen pounds during those two weeks, and I just felt exhausted. It was a complete shock to my whole body. I still had a lot of pain in my chest and ribs from the LUCAS machine (a mechanical chest compression machine). The ICD (implantable cardioverter-defibrillator) was also going to take 4–6 weeks to heal. I used this time to get closer to God. When I was discharged, they told me I could not lift more than five pounds with my left arm because of the ICD. They changed my blood pressure meds, added aspirin daily, and that was it. For about a month I did not do much physically.

After about a month I started going back to the gym. I just wanted to start off with some light cardio and light lifting. That was the time that PTSD really kicked in. I knew I had to get my strength back to be able to go back to work. I started with light cardio on the exercise bike and light lifting. All that was running through my head was this ICD going to shock me. Am I just going to collapse and die right there? I read about the ICD and I found out that if it goes off, it is going to really hurt. Through prayer I was able to progress, and I was able to work out everything except my chest. During this time, I was focusing on trying to build my body back up, reading the Bible, watching videos about God, praying, and wondering why God revived me.

My goal was to build up my body as well as I could to get back to work. I had a solid 165-pound body before the cardiac arrest. I was 150 pounds, very weak, and still in pain after a few weeks. I was told my ribs were going to hurt for two months. With the help of God, I built up myself good enough to get back to work in April. During this time a part of me still felt like I was in the spirit world.

John 1:1–2

1: In the beginning was the Word, and the Word was with God, and the Word was God.
2: He was in the beginning with God.

I keep saying it, but God's Word is **very** powerful. You should talk to God all the time. Just start talking to him every day and he will put you on the narrow path that leads to Him.

Back to Work

While working I kept worrying about the ICD going off. I was a supervisor at a hardware store so there was a lot of walking and a good number of lifting products up. I was not worried about dying, just getting shocked. It took a few weeks for me to get used to being back to work. I felt like I went back a month too soon. I still was not feeling like myself. Every day I could not wait to get home to spend time with God. I love learning about God, and I love to read the Bible. I was spending 2–3 hours a day watching different YouTube videos, watching different sermons, reading the Bible, basically anything that I could learn more about God. God gave the foundation of knowledge, but it was up to me to understand it. I always get certain feelings about how God feels about certain things, but I always want to find out the reason why. Reading the Bible is the best way for me to converse with God. That is why I read the Bible constantly, because God tells me something different each time. God's Word means everything to me. Now it is a passion of mine. Writing takes away from that sometimes. All I can do is focus on God and keep moving forward the best I can.

Matthew 4:4

4: But he answered, "It is written, 'Man shall not live by bread alone, but by every word that comes from the mouth of God.'"

I remember one day I was on my way to work, and I was looking around at the cars, buildings, and people thinking to myself none of these matters. This life is a blink of an eye compared to eternity. I could feel angels in the clouds and all around, the one thing missing was the most important. The worship of God. I saw masses of people kneeling while praying to God. They gave him praise, worship, and glory. It was beautiful. If everyone felt God, they would immediately fall to their knees and start worshipping our Lord. After the vision I still felt the angels all around. I could not see them, but I felt their presence. God has truly blessed me. God wants you to believe his word. It is all true. The Father, Son, and Holy Spirit are so loving, and God is frustrated that more people do not even try to talk to him, read about him, or try to know him. God literally speaks things into existence. Just think of that for a minute. I also had days where I would see my sins and get very upset. I was very emotional for the first year. A lot of the depression came from knowing how I felt in heaven. I felt home and I was extremely happy in the presence of Jesus Christ. That is my home. I am no longer a part of this world. Jesus said the same exact thing. This is Satan's world and I want no part of it. Then I got to the point where I said to myself, I have a job to do here. Stop being a baby and fight this war for the glory of God. This world is a literal war for souls. It is the most powerful and meaningful war that will ever happen. Now I am a soldier in God's army. I do what God tells me, without hesitation.

Many people say that Bibles are man-made and have different translations and meanings. They do not realize that God uses people to do his will. The person who was writing those words was being guided by the Holy Spirit. So, every word in the Bible is written by God. Another thing that people do not realize when there are different versions or translations, God wants a person to interpret or understand it the way it is presented to each person. There is a reason for everything. God did not make any mistakes and he wants everyone to know it.

As the year went on, I kept getting stronger and stronger. I was also getting those episodes more frequently. In 2019, I was getting episodes 1–2 times a day. Then I got anemia which did not help anything. This was when the device came into the picture. I started noticing that during these episodes my heart rhythm was all over the place. My heart would start beating fast and then just drop and go very low. My device would detect it and raise my heart rate. It never hurt when it would raise my heart rate, but I knew it. When they test the device they raise my heart rate just a few beats per minute, so I know what it feels like. The ICD also records everything, so now they were seeing every time it happened. The episodes were painful. I would start getting a slight pain in my upper left chest. Then, after about forty-five seconds, I would get a bad pain in my chest. Sometimes it got severe and would go into my left shoulder and arm. I would always grab my wrist to feel my heart rate. I knew if it went too high or lowI would get shocked. So, it was around August of 2019 that the device would occasionally raise my heart rate and then the episode stopped. It always lasted 3–5 minutes. My cardiologist kept doing different tests and they could not find the cause. All I could do was pray every time I would not get shocked, and believe me, I did.

At this point, in January 2020, I felt like I was losing the battle. The episodes were happening more and more frequently. I was thinking that God gave me more time to spend with my son and now God was going to take me home for good. My faith never swayed, I was just so tired mentally and physically that I did not know how much more I could take. The episodes now started happening at the gym or with any strenuous activity. On January 13, 2020, I was off from work. I slept in late, and I was just laying down. At around 12:00 p.m. I started getting an episode. I remember I was curled up in my bed and I was praying. I could feel my heart fluttering, stopping the racing. Then in a split second everything got dark; I was gone. I woke up and my heart hurt so bad. I did not feel the shock, but I knew I was shocked. I never felt my entire heart hurt like that. I laid down a little longer to see if it was going to happen again. I got up and got dressed. I hate going to hospitals, so I did not go. I had to run an errand and then went to my cardiologist. They took me right in. I got hooked up to the machine and they said, "Yes, it went off; but that's what it is for."

A few of the cardiologists looked at the event and decided to put me on a different medication. It was antiarrhythmic to try and prevent the episodes. I did not have a problem with it, the only problem was I had to be put in the hospital for four days. It was sort of a last resort medication. They thought electrical impulses in my heart were the problem. At this point I was willing to try anything. They were going to set that up.

Later that day I went to the market. I got what I needed, then I was just going to go home and lay down. For some reason after a shock, I would feel like I had no energy. I was driving home, and I felt another episode coming. I started to get scared. I did not want to pass out while I was driving. I started to pull over, but I knew I had a little more time. I got to a light, it just turned red, but I kept going. I knew it was coming. I pulled into the first parking lot I saw. Everything started to get dark. I stopped the car and put it in park. While all this was happening, I really thought I was going to die. As soon as I put the car in park everything went black, and I was out. I woke up and slammed on the brake and tried to put the car in park, but I had already done it before I passed out. I knew it was another shock. I really did not know what to do, I honestly thought I was dying. I eventually drove home. I was keeping track of everything. I just knew that two shocks in one day was not good.

Over the next few months, I did not get shocked anymore. I was still getting episodes on a regular basis though. I went into the hospital to get put on the antiarrhythmic medication. I did not have any episodes in the hospital. I looked at this as a new start. I was hoping the medication would work and I could live my life without any of those problems. I went about my life as I normally do. I was really hoping that this medication would work. About a week later after I started, the episodes were still there. I was very frustrated at that point. The only thing I could do is trust God and keep moving forward.

The Last Stand

At this time, I was feeling defeated. I made it all this way, I kept working, working out, and spending time with God. On the other hand, I did not think God brought me all this way to die now. There was still something more that God wanted me to do. The fight went on. On May 15, 2020, I was at work, just doing normal things and I felt an episode coming on. I went up to the break room. I put my arms on the table, put my head on my arms and was just praying. Suddenly, I see a bright light and feel 3,000 volts of electricity hit my heart in a split second. My arms went straight out; I had my work phone in my hand and that went flying. I let out a groan and it all happened within a second. This was the first shock that I did not pass out first, so I felt it. They do really hurt. I would rather pass out first. I panicked, grabbed my stuff, and just left and went home. I was so tired. I called work and told them why I had to leave. I did not want to go to the hospital. I called the doctor on call. He called me back and told me to increase one of my heart meds and if it went off again, I had to go to the hospital. He advised me to go then, but I wouldn't go. The next day I had six bad episodes. I really could not take it anymore. I was too tired to do anything. I felt like I was dying. I just do not like going to the hospital, I hate it. I was praying to God, and I told him I cannot handle it. I told God if it goes off again that I am going to go to the hospital. At least they could make me comfortable. I just kept praying. I told God that I am very tired, and I am not afraid of dying, I just do not want to suffer. Shortly after that I was shocked again. I called the doctor on call and told him, and I asked what hospital to go to. He told me to go to Miriam Hospital, he told me to call 911 and the ambulance came and took me to the hospital. As soon as I got into the ambulance I felt at peace, this is where God wanted me to be.

When I got to the hospital, they were waiting for me. They immediately took me in and started putting IVs in me. Then I got a call from the doctor. He asked me where I was. I told him I am where you told me to go. He told me that he talked to the other cardiologist, and they were going to do surgery on my heart, but I had to go to RI Hospital because they are the only ones that could do it. He said I am getting transferred. Miriam gave me some medication to help me to relax and within a few hours I was at RI Hospital. Once there they hooked me up to almost everything. They even put the pads on me for the external defibrillator even though I had the ICD in my chest. They had to do a COVID test before putting me in a room, so I had to wait a few hours. During that time, I started getting an episode. All the alarms started going off and a bunch of doctors came running in. I started laughing and told them this happens all the time. The good thing was that when I was getting an episode in the hospital, they would immediately do an EKG while I had the episode. I did not think much about it at the time, but it turned out to be very important.

I was put in a room in the cardiac intensive care unit. They gave me medication to relax me and pain meds because my chest would hurt for a day or two whenever I got shocked. I was finally able to relax. I knew I was in the best possible place for what was going on and I knew all of this was God's will. I was told that they were going to do cardiac ablation surgery, they just had to do a PET scan before they did the surgery. I was all for it. I had gotten worse and worse. It was now easy to see what caused the cardiac arrest, but they still did not have a diagnosis. The cardiac ablation surgery was still just basically a guess. There was no proof that it was going to change anything. At this point they were out of options. Monday came and went, and they did not do the test. They said it was going to take a few days. Everything happens for a reason. I was still getting episodes. All the alarms would go off and about six people would come in. I was giving a play-by-play of what was happening. That Wednesday, around 7:00 p.m., I got an episode. They immediately hooked me up to an EKG. I was telling them what was happening. After a couple minutes I told them the ICD was going to go off. Ten seconds later . . . those 3,000 volts hit my heart and I was sitting up and I went straight back into the bed holding my chest. That one really hurt. They gave me Valium and the nurse came over and gave me morphine. She said, "That was really scary." I could see it affected her a little. I am thinking to myself these people see a lot of things all the time, so for that to affect a nurse in the cardiac ICU, it has to be bad. I just go through it every day. God just gave me the strength to get through it for years.

I was at the point that I could not take it anymore. Every time I got shocked it took everything out of me. The multiple episodes every day and now getting shocked all the time, I was done. I was ready to die. I was praying and asking God, "What more must I go through? If I am going to die, please take me now." I was serious with my prayers; at that point, I had enough. If they could not find the cause or stop them, I wanted to die. I was suffering. I just kept praying. God only gives us what we can handle. . . then just a little more to make us stronger. Once we meet the point where we cannot go any further God takes over and helps us. He does this to show us that anything is possible with God. We must trust him. I still had 100 percent faith and trust in God, I just did not want to suffer anymore. Looking back, it has given me so much strength. I would suffer through anything for the love of God. That was my moment. That is when God saw that I would go to him and trust him no matter how bad the storm got. I prayed to God to take the pain away, live life without these episodes. God always comes through. When it is his timing and his will. God does everything for a reason. God was strengthening my faith. I could go through torture, any physical pain, and my Lord and Savior, Jesus Christ, will always be with me and get me through it. I fear nothing living in Jesus, except God.

The good thing about being in the hospital, with the monitors and the EKG recording the whole events, allowed the team of cardiologists to finally figure out the problem. They did the PET scan but canceled the surgery. I still had no idea what was going on yet. That Friday they switched my heart medication to diltiazem. I did not have any episodes that day. The next day they put me on the extended-release diltiazem. My heart medication was needed, so I hit the button and told them my medication was due. Well, this went on for two hours. I was starting to get chest pain. I was hooked up on everything, so I could not go tell them I needed my heart med. Finally, the nurse came in and I was so frustrated I was arguing with the nurse. While I was arguing with her, I got my last episode. It was not a bad one, but I was still aggravated. I knew it wouldn't have happened if I got my medication on time.

That is when the doctor came in. He talked to me for twenty minutes and apologized at least ten times during the conversation because they knew what was wrong but waited to put me on the correct medication. He said they figured it out during one of my episodes when they took the EKG. I guess in the middle of the week they had the diagnosis, but my medication did not get changed until Friday. Finally, after four years, a cardiac arrest, getting shocked eight times, and hundreds of episodes, they figured it out. I get coronary artery spasms. When it goes into spasm it basically cuts the blood supply to my heart. It feels like a heart attack, it causes my heart to go into atrial fibrillation and my heart beats so fast that it's basically not doing anything. Then either the spasms stop, and I am fine, or I go into A-fib and then my heart just stops. He said it is not common here in the United States, it's more common in Europe. It is treated by calcium channel blockers and nitrates. I am on a lot of diltiazem. He told me to take as much as I can until my blood pressure gets too low, and I am on an extended release of nitrate. I also have nitroglycerin to take if I start to get a spasm. As of right now, I am so thankful to God that I do not have to deal with the spasms anymore.

Revelation from God

So now I am in the hospital for the last night, and I am going home in the morning. I was praying to God and thanking him that this is over. It was at that point I got a revelation from God. He told me that now is the time to tell my story, along with the things he has strong feelings about. It was a relief in two ways. I found out what the problem is and now I know why God revived me. I needed these three years to put everything together and now it was all completely clear to me. Tell everyone the miracle God did and get the message out about certain things God wants addressed.

God Comes Through Again

As I take my walk with God, I am constantly facing physical challenges. I honestly thought that I was going to be good physically after all that. Then I got hit by another storm of physical problems. In April of 2022, I had to face two different things at the same time. My iron-deficiency anemia returned. Shortly after that, I was bench pressing, the same way I have for ten years, as I was pushing the weight up, I heard and felt cracking in my right shoulder. I then, by habit, brought the bar back down for one more rep, and I heard and felt the cracking on the way up. I struggled to finish that rep. After that, I had no strength in my right shoulder and the pain really started. It took two months to finally get an MRI. Because of my ICD they had to have someone come from the company and put the device in safe mode. The MRI showed a "high-grade bursal surface tear." At that point I needed four infusions for the anemia and surgery for my shoulder. I worked for two months with both issues, which was a miracle. The last time I had anemia, I was out of work for a month. Because of the amount of damage to my shoulder, I should not have been able to work. I am not getting into everything, but there were four different problems with my shoulder; it wasn't just a tear. I was so tired, my muscles hurt. My shoulder was in pain so I would normally not have been able to work with all the problems. I knew I was going to need time off for the surgery and rehab, I needed to save as much time as possible for that. If I was out of work for a month before, and 2–3 months after, I could have lost my job and disability income. It only lasts for about three months.

I was originally upset and aggravated that both things happened. Then, I realized I needed time to write this second edition. I was too tired to write or read anything with the anemia. Everything happens for a reason. It is fine to get aggravated or upset about something. It is a sign to turn to God. I told God how I felt, then put everything in his hands. He got me through it. It allowed me to get closer to Jesus Christ. Shortly after I got back to work, I got the dream and then the vision. After that, I started to feel one with God. I just want to live for him. I trust God with everything, and I am finally at peace with my life.

Depression and PTSD

God wants me to go over the depression and PTSD that I go through. The more we know about certain things, the better we can understand things that people may be going through that we cannot see from the outside. With everything that I went through, everything I felt and saw, and the knowledge I was given, it is very easy to ask, "Why are you depressed?" There were so many emotions I was feeling when I got home. I still felt the spirit world and God's love, but there were many questions running through my head. I did not know what caused the cardiac arrest at that time, so I was wondering how I died. I had an even bigger question running through my head which was, "Why did I live?" How can someone die for over a half hour and walk out of the hospital two weeks later with virtually no sign it even happened. It felt so loving and beautiful being with Jesus, I was very upset that I was sent back. Once you experience his love as a spirit along with no negative feelings at all, then you will understand.

Some can go crazy sitting there and wonder why didn't God just keep me there. I felt God's love very strongly, so I used that to help me through very dark times. I started a journal that I would write every day and that helped with the emotions. I am just sitting here, with this thing in my chest, having all these feelings from God about the Catholic church and thinking about how sinful I am. Tears running down my face begging God to tell me why I lived. I could feel God's love, but being here, I had all these negative feelings attacking me. When you are in the spirit world with God, you feel his love. At the same time, you do not feel pain, physical or emotional, there is no worrying, nothing to be afraid of and nothing negative. Try to imagine everything negative in your life gone and only feel God's love, it's so peaceful and wonderful. At the same time. I was not looking at the big picture. I was being selfish and not thinking that there was a reason why all of it happened. It took me almost a month to be able to look at it from a different point of view. I just proved that there is a God. He is real and loving. Science can never explain what happened to me. Science tells me my brain starts dying within a few minutes without oxygen. From the time I hit the floor, 911 being called, then getting to the house was almost ten minutes. It is scientifically impossible that I am alive and fully functioning mentally and physically for the length of time I was dead. Nobody had a stopwatch, but it was approximately 30–40 minutes that I was dead.

Before this happened, I was working out 4–5 days a week for five years. Around the two-month period the depression got a little better and I started going back to the gym. This is when PTSD kicked in. I started thinking I was going to drop dead, or the ICD was going to go off. When I went back to work it just got worse. Then the nightmares started. Once they started, I had trouble sleeping. I was having nightmares about different ways of me dying. An example was when I had a nightmare that someone stabbed me in my thigh. I could feel the blood pouring out of the artery and everything started to get dark, then I woke up sweating. Some nights I could not remember the nightmare, I would just wake up frightened and sweating. That made the depression worse and during the day I would struggle with the device going off. It was a vicious circle. I finally mentioned it to my doctor, and he put me on Wellbutrin. After several weeks it really did help. I did not have nightmares, the PTSD during the day calmed down, and I was in a better mood.

I was able to focus on God, work, and working out. I was reading the Bible for the second time and my relationship with God just kept getting better. I accepted the fact that God would do his will through me at his timing, not mine. I was in a good place. I was writing different Bible verses that God wanted me to write down. I knew they were important but at the time I did not know why (all those Bible verses were used for this book). Then the ICD started going off. Almost immediately it caused me to have panic attacks; my depression and PTSD got worse. Now I was afraid the device was going to go off all the time. I remember being at the gym and doing bench presses. I would think what would happen if I got shocked while bench pressing 250 pounds. I started thinking that every time I get an episode my device is going to go off. My doctor increased the Wellbutrin for panic attacks.

I still had issues with all of it, but the medication did help, and I was focusing so much on God, work, and working out that the days were flying by. I kept saying to myself that this is God's will. This is exactly what God wants to happen right now and I really put everything in his hands. That is how I am. God does know what is going on. If he wants to intervene, he will. The one thing I stopped saying and I hate hearing is, "Why me?" My answer to that is why not me.

Romans 8:31

31: What then shall we say to these things? If God is for us, who can be against us?

Psalm 34:17–18

17: When the righteous cry for help, the LORD hears and delivers them out of all their troubles.
18: The LORD is near to the brokenhearted and saves the crushed in spirit.

It is not always going to be easy, but God gives us the tools, love, and strength to get through anything.

For those who say that "God never helps me" or "God does not care about me," the answer is simple: You do not know Jesus Christ. If you are in Christ, you do not hold onto the painful things forever. I still have issues with depression, PTSD, and panic attacks. God works through other people to help us. I see a doctor that makes it so much easier for me. Yes, I am on medication for it, but there is nothing wrong with that. I made the mistake of not getting help the first year after the cardiac arrest. They did not tell me about PTSD or depression when I was in the hospital. It is possible they did before my memory came back, but it was still up to me to get help. Why do you think God gives some people the ambition and gift of being a good doctor? God thinks of everything. All these issues are terrible and if you have any mental health issues, I urge you to get help from a doctor. It is nothing to fool around with. I still struggle with PTSD, anxiety, depression, and nightmares. Unfortunately, that is a part of my life now. I talk to God and that gets me through it. When it gets bad, he is the only one that helps. Sometimes we go through something that nobody else can relate to unless they went through the same thing. God puts people in place to help people. Ultimately, it is all God because he gave people the ambition, the gifts, the ability, and the life to be in that situation to help. These issues must be addressed. I do not want to be in a position where I do not feel anything. I always lean on Jesus. PTSD can take over. It is scary. My heart goes out to those that are going through it without having Jesus in their life. I will not even think about what I would do if I did not have Jesus. God is everything to me. Once you get to that point, that is when you start to hear God speak to you. You feel the Holy Spirit stepping in, so you stay on the narrow path. You must try every day to get that relationship. I am blessed because God has been like that with me since I got home from the hospital. Anyone can reach that level with God. You must want it. The biggest trigger for my PTSD is sometimes I feel that God wants more out of me or I am failing at what God wants me to do. The other trigger is once you have felt the love of Jesus Christ while in his presence, that's all you want. This life is difficult. Being a Christian is not easy. You must be carrying the light of God all of the time. We are living in a world that hates us and we know we are no longer of this world. But I have to look at it for what it is. The world hates God, the world hates Jesus, and if you're a truly saved Christian, the world hates you too. I look at it as a badge of honor. Something that really helped me emotionally and mentally is the tattoo I got. I have a big tattoo on my right forearm that everyone can see. It says *"Jesus"*; in the middle, it says, *"The Way The Truth The Life."* It is therapy for me because everyone can see I love Jesus. It's a good talking point. Many people have commented on it. I want the world to know I am a servant of Jesus and, even if it means death, I will happily die for my love for God. I did not get it to walk around and think I am better than any other Christian. I have a story to tell. I want people to ask me about it, so I can share with them the miracles Jesus does. I must be the light in the darkness. I have felt the love of God while being in his presence. It is something I want everyone to feel. Also, I see a lot of people at my job. A few thousands a day. I cannot run up to them and tell them about our Lord and Savior, rather they approach me about it. I average one person a day that I tell my story to because of that tattoo.

Trust me, I had a few days that I was just depressed. I would talk to God. I would ask him, "What is all this for? Nothing changed in my life, except more things going wrong. It would have been so much easier if you had just kept me there. No more physical pain or emotional struggle. How much do I have to go through?" That is when I would get the answer; God would say, "It is not all about you. There are more things involved. If you look through the Bible, it was many years of suffering for many of God's people. You will no longer be the one needing help to get through your days. You will have an overabundance and it will be other people that need help from you. You will deliver, in the name of God, because you know how it feels to need. If you never go through that, how can you relate to someone else that is sick, dying, the world is against them, they have no hope, but then you arrive." Everything God has taught you becomes real, and you give them hope, in God's name, then it is on to the next one God sends to you. So, we must love and trust God. His strongest servants are the ones that overcame the most in this life. God can trust them because we do not doubt our God.

Now, I have the added element of my body that keeps breaking down. I was very surprised when I was just doing something that I have been doing on a regular basis for ten years, and a tendon just snapped. The anemia that I have is also something that is going to happen on a regular basis. Whenever I get back into the gym now I have to worry about a tendon just snapping out of nowhere. My depression got worse while dealing with my injury and anemia at the same time. I cannot tell how many infusions worked because I cannot go to the gym or go to work. I just must face the fact that these physical problems are going to be a regular part of my life. It just gets difficult when I cannot do very much physically. I know that there are more things that I have to learn, and part of this has to do with getting this book done. There are things that I have to be better at as far as going to church, learning more and more to get out there and do God's work. This is a learning phase for me. Even with everything that I went through, God was still refining me and letting me know that there is more than I can do. I am going to be honest, being a Christian is very difficult, but worth it in the end. I want to be honest. This second book contains so much more information. It tells the truth about many things. God wants this book completed. It may cause controversy, but it is the truth.

I struggled for six months with the anemia and then the surgery. It takes 6–12 months to fully heal. I got through it and was able to complete this book in the process. Now I am just listening for God. My focus is getting this book published. It will help some people. I am back at work, back in the gym, and just taking it one day at a time. I know I am close to something changing in my life soon. I got the dream and vision from Jesus. He wanted to let me know that he is putting me in the right situation. I am very excited about the future.

And Then . . . After All of That, I Got COVID

Once again, I thought things were turning around. I was working out at about 50–60 percent of my normal weight, I was getting bigger and stronger, and I got clearance from my surgeon that I could lift what I could handle. I was excited to finally get the green light, then I got COVID. I was fighting through a sinus infection that would not go away. I got it in December of 2022 and now it was March of 2023. I saw my ENT doctor and I had to get a CT scan of my sinuses. I already had two surgeries ten years before this. I was on four different antibiotics from a walk-in clinic, and they said no more antibiotics. That was the only thing that made me feel better. So I had the CT scan scheduled, but I felt awful. I was off antibiotics for about two weeks. I said to myself, I will just go to the urgent care down the street, and I will not say anything about the previous place I went to. I went there and they said I had to take a COVID test before I could be seen. That was normal, they did that everywhere. They took the swab and said they will call me after the results so I can be seen. They called me to go in, so I thought, but I had COVID, the doctor called me an hour later. He said with my heart issues that I was a "high risk" and he called in medication for COVID and gave me antibiotics for my sinus infection. Take it from me, you will always need God. The good thing is that God always wants us to need him, pray to him, worship him. Imagine if he was mean. I am grateful that my God wants me to need him. That is why it is so upsetting to him that our country does not want him. We need God. Everything is getting worse. We must repent and beg for forgiveness. I can assure you we are out of time.. We were all given our chances. Things are in motion. Jesus is coming.

CHAPTER 3

THE LOVE OF GOD

I felt God's love very strongly from the cardiac arrest until about two months after I got home. I still feel it, but it is not as strong. It is impossible to explain. You do not want or need anything else while in the presence of God. It is something you feel throughout your whole soul and mind. It consumes you and I cannot wait to feel it again. I can understand why hell feels so tortuous and painful. Hell is the complete absence of God. I truly get upset for the souls that are going there and will never feel the love of God.

Psalm 36:7

7: How precious is your steadfast love, O God! The children of mankind take refuge in the shadow of your wings.

1 John 4:9–10

9: In this the love of God was made manifest among us, that God sent his only Son into the world, so that we might live through him.
10: In this is love, **not that we have loved God but that he loved us** and sent his Son to be the propitiation for our sins.

1 John 4:16

16: So we have come to know and to believe the love that God has for us. God is love, and whoever abides in love abides in God, and God abides in him.

That is a very strong love. When you feel it, you feel the love that God has for us is also protection; you feel extremely safe. For the Father to send his only Son to die for us. For Jesus to willingly do the Father's will to be crucified and die for us, it's a love we cannot comprehend. It is so beautiful and amazing to just think how blessed we are to have a God that loves us that much. Also think about that without Jesus Christ we all would be in hell where we all belong. To know God, you must know that and accept it.

I knew I would be safe when I died because I felt God's love running through me. I knew once I heard Jesus tell me, "I am the Way, the Truth, and the Life"; that was one of the messages he wanted me to get out to everyone. All of humanity relied on Jesus rising from the dead. Without that, then we have nothing. I can attest to the fact that Jesus did rise from the dead and that Jesus is the savior of the world, not some prophet. While in his presence, Jesus made me feel so loved. I cannot compare it to any emotion, feeling, or anything here on earth to compare it to. There are a lot of painful things that happen in our lives. Death of loved ones, physical or emotional abuse, divorces, breakups, shootings, murders, rapes, the worst thing you have ever been through, and I can tell you without any pause or doubt that it's worth it to be able to feel the love of God. The problem is that I cannot compare it to anything. I have been through a lot in my life, which could be why God chose me, and his love is worth all of that pain multiplied 1,000 times, to be blessed enough to feel that love that only God can give you.

When I got out of the hospital, God's love was what gave me ambition to get back to normal. I could feel his love and I still felt the spirit world, but I knew that it was going to go away. I had all this knowledge running around in my head and I did not know how to understand it. But I had this huge thirst for God. I wanted to read the Bible and watch videos to understand this knowledge. That is why it took a few years for it to make sense. I was reading the Bible every night and watching sermons on YouTube. I would watch sermons and debates from Apologia Church. I really like their views and I can see how God works through them. I would watch debates between different religions.

The reason why I brought that up is because God's love penetrates through everything. It is very strong. The one place God blocks out his love is hell. I am praying that if you do not know Jesus that you will repent, start reading the Bible, and put all your energy to know Jesus.

One thing that really irritates me is when people say, "Well, I am going to hell anyway," when they refer to something stupid. If they went to hell for ten seconds, it would be the longest ten seconds of their life, and they would be begging to know Jesus. I can tell you that our minds cannot comprehend hell. If we see it, in this physical state, you could die immediately. People just should not joke about it. It is real and terrifying. I do not love God because I want to go to heaven. I love God because I want to be with him. That's all I want. I will be perfectly happy being with God forever. Some people can relate to that, and some people cannot. If you want to go to heaven to just see your loved ones that died or because you do not want to suffer in hell, then you do not know God, never mind loving him.

Luke 14:26

26: "If anyone comes to me and does not hate his own father and mother and wife and children and brothers and sisters, yes, and even his own life, he cannot be my disciple.

I can already hear it: "Wait, we are supposed to love everyone, or Jesus did not really mean that?" I keep saying how powerful God's Word is. We are all sinners and God is a holy God without sin. God hates sin. We must realize how dirty we really are. We sin every day, multiple times. We are not clean until we are cleansed by the blood of Jesus Christ. We are enemies of God until we are saved. Also, God will not be second to ANYONE. If you love someone more than God, pray to God for guidance. God wants us to talk, pray, and worship him.

I have a son. My father passed away and he was a devoted Catholic. He said the rosary every day. I love my father regardless of his religion (we are going over the Catholic religion soon). I also accept whatever judgment God has for him. I love my son, but I love God more because God created him, guides him, and protects him. God's love for my son is something I could never match. There is absolutely nobody or nothing that is above God for me. Once you reach that point you are truly in Christ. If you're having trouble with this, that's OK. It takes a lot to reach this point. I'd recommend praying to God about it. Pray for understanding and help. Repent and pray. Also, write down Bible verses that are related to this and read them every day. I did that a lot after the cardiac arrest. It is something I must start doing again.

Since I went over hell before, I must go over heaven. All I can tell you from direct experience is that it is beautiful. When I died, I felt heaven, but it was secondary to Jesus Christ. It is more about what you do not feel. You do not feel the weight of sin or anything evil. I have visions of heaven. One vision I have is the water of life. There are angels all around it. That is one of the places people go when they first arrive. They are cleaned and the water has life in them. Just as the tree of life. That is the thing about God. He is love, life, and holy. The problem is that we are sinful and dirty. We must have no sin and be cleansed to be able to be in this perfect place. From the knowledge God gave me explains heaven. When you're in the spirit world your emotions are much stronger along with having much more knowledge. I read a book called *A Divine Revelation of Heaven* by Mary Kay Baxter. I did not see most of those things that she saw in heaven, but they have been explained to me by God. This is what happens when I read certain things, I can see it and I know it's true. I could feel the peace, but the love of Jesus Christ overpowered a lot of it. With being in the spirit world the biggest thing I noticed was the knowledge that you have there. You just know everything about God, the Father, Jesus Christ, and the Holy Spirit. You just know that they are real, and God created everything. They say that we use 10 percent of our brain capacity. It feels like 100 percent in the spirit world. Just like the love God has for us, I cannot explain how I knew so much. Just like when I got home from the hospital, I knew that being able to feel God's love and being in the spirit world would leave me eventually.

The good thing is that I did not lose the knowledge God gave me. I may not know why something is wrong or right, but I just know. Every time that happens, I can validate it from the Bible. Sometimes I will be watching YouTube and it would be a sermon or someone talking about God, and I know if what they're saying was the truth or not. I know many preachers that are not teaching God's Word. They are using God's words for their own benefit. They do it because they value money over anything else. They make it a watered-down version of God's Word. They make it look like he is all forgiving and loving and nobody is going to hell. They say that they have this magic prayer or walk up to you and heal your pain and, suddenly, people are "saved." That is not loving God. I also noticed I can feel the Holy Spirit in certain people. It is a strong feeling I get.

Matthew 24:11–13

11: And many false prophets will arise and lead many astray.

12: And because lawlessness will be increased, the love of many will grow cold.

13: But the one who endures to the end will be saved.

Acts 5:27–29

27: And when they had brought them, they sent them before the council. And the high priest question them,

28: saying, "We strictly charged you not to teach in this name, yet here you have filled through them with your teaching, and you intend to bring this man's blood upon us."

29: But Peter and the apostles answered, "We must obey God rather than men.

Acts 5:40–42

40: and when they had called in the apostles, they beat them and charged them not to speak in the name of Jesus, and let them go.

41: Then they left the presence of the council, rejoicing that they were counted worthy to suffer dishonor for the name.

42: And every day, in the temple and from house to house, they did not cease teaching and preaching that the Christ is Jesus.

After Jesus was crucified, died, and then raised up on the third day, the apostles could feel that strong love. They kept preaching about God and the resurrection of Jesus, but the government made it a crime. They felt the love so strong from Jesus that they were happy that they got beat up for preaching about Jesus. I can understand that. I would never hide my faith in God no matter what the cost is.

Whether it be torture, death, or the death of others. I would be honored to die for my faith in Jesus. That is how strong God's love is. People may look at that and think I am crazy, or I am just saying it. Some people think I might fold and deny Christ if it meant my life. To that I would say that you have not felt his love that strong. I keep saying how depressed I was because I did not want to come back. So why would I ever delay feeling that again?

From the day of the cardiac arrest, my life completely changed in several different ways. The love and protection of God affects me every day. My relationship with God is like nothing else. I can feel that he is always here with me. I put everything in God's hands. I am always getting revelations. What that is, God will reveal to me a truth I did not know before. I will give you one example. I told myself that I was going to read the book of Revelation until I understood all of it. With the seven seals that only Jesus could open, I was getting confused with the sixth seal. I told God I did not understand it. The way I was reading it would contradict everything I knew about the Rapture. After I told God and prayed, I read it again, and it made perfect sense. You will understand when you read it later in the book. I will explain everything. So those are revelations I get from God. God also gave me another one. God just put it in my head and explained it. Sometimes I get a revelation that its meaning is for me to emphasize certain things. Some are just meant for me. I constantly pray for more information, more revelations, and more dreams. I want to know everything I possibly can about God.

Some days I just feel overwhelmed. When it first hit me about the anemia and the surgery, I was upset. I was thinking about how the shoulder surgery is going to take 6–12 months to fully heal. After a week of being upset and wrestling with God, I remembered something. I tell God that I will do whatever he wants me to do. I am thinking about doing things to help people find Jesus, not surgery. I realized that this is what God wants me to do. Now I have an idea why, but it does not matter. I must be strong and get through this the best I can. Then there might be something else after.

How Can You Feel God's Love Now?

To be honest, feeling God's love 100 percent here is very difficult. That is between God and you. There are ways that you can feel God's love very strongly here on earth though. When you have a group and they are all praying and worshipping God together, you will feel it. I've only been to one Christian church. In situations like that I can feel it. There are many people that have felt it all in different ways. The day that the Holy Spirit comes upon you, and you're born again, you can feel it. I am very sensitive when it comes to the Holy Spirit. When I was growing up and going to a Catholic church, I never felt anything, until I started feeling negative feelings. When I first walked into a Christian church, I immediately felt the presence of the Holy Spirit. The best way is when you're in a group where everybody is worshipping God.

CHAPTER 4

FALSE RELIGIONS

Satan has worked very hard, from the beginning, to turn or trick people away from the one and only true God. The one true God consists of three persons: the Father, the Son, and the Holy Spirit. God was not created, nor any of the persons of God. They were here from the beginning, and they will always be here. God knows of no other God. None was created before him or after him. The crazy thing is that the demons knew Jesus was God and humans don't.

Matthew 8:28–29

28: And when he came to the other side, to the country of the Gadarenes, two demon- possessed men met him, coming out of the tombs, so fierce that no one could pass that way.
29: And behold, they cry it out, "What have you to do with us, O Son of God? Have you come here to torment us before the time?"

Just think of that for a minute. Demons knew that Jesus Christ was the Son of God. There is one simple explanation. If God does not reveal the truth, people will stand in front of God and they will have a big surprise. If you show no interest in knowing God, then that is your fault. That is your free will to not want to know God. That is why I always say salvation is between God and each person. I do know that the road is very narrow that leads to Jesus. I see it every day. About 90 percent of the people I see each day have no clue what is coming. And I see about 1,000 people a day.

The Word Became Flesh

John 1:1–5

1: In the beginning was the Word, and the Word was with God, and the Word was God.
2: He was in the beginning with God.
3: All things were made through him, and without him was not anything made that was made.
4: In him was life, and no life was the light of men.
5: The light shines in the darkness, and the darkness has not overcome it.

Now when we get into John 1, this is clearly telling everyone that Jesus Christ was with the Father from the beginning and that everything that was made was made through Jesus Christ. Satan was created by God through Jesus Christ, so that clearly shows Mormonism is a false religion, along with Islam and Judaism. These religions claim that Jesus Christ was a mighty prophet. Jesus sent me a revelation about this theory. Just for a second let's say that Jesus was a prophet. Why would God the Father constantly give him revelations even though Jesus Christ was teaching everyone that he is God? If John the Baptist was claiming that he was God, God would stop sending him revelations. These religions' saying that Jesus Christ is a prophet is false because he said multiple times that he is God. Jesus told the high priest that "before Abraham was, I Am." Anyone that is remotely familiar with the Old Testament knows God refers to himself as "I Am."

Before anyone starts claiming their religion is correct, they have to answer these three questions: "If Jesus was just a prophet, why did he keep telling everyone that he is God? Why would God the Father keep giving Jesus Christ the power to do the many miracles that he performed? Why would God the Father keep giving Jesus information if he was only a prophet?" Jesus raised multiple people from the dead, the waters of the sea listened to him, he was able to feed thousands of people with hardly any food and after Jesus gave up his spirit there was a massive earthquake. The sky darkened and dead Christians rose from the dead and started preaching in the cities. As you read through each of these false religions, please answer those questions. One last thing, please read a Bible that is available before Joseph Smith and Muhammad. (7) The first widespread edition of the Bible was assembled by St, Jerome around AD 400. This manuscript included all thirty-nine books of the Old Testament and the twenty-seven books of the New Testament in the same language: Latin.

It is plainly obvious that it is easier for you to believe a false religion that you were brought up with. It is more difficult to go against what you have been taught. I was brought up in a false religion. I did not have a problem wiping out everything that I believed before and read the Bible with a clear head. In the end, this is your life, it is your soul, and the ultimate question is: "Do you want to be with God in heaven or do you want to take a huge chance of going to hell for eternity?" The choice is yours.

Roman Catholic Religion

I grew up in a Catholic household. I received all my sacraments and followed it the best I could. As I got older, every time I went to church, something just felt wrong. I did not like calling the priest "Father." I didn't like going to confession either, so I only went once to fulfill a fake sacrament. I asked myself, "Why should I confess my sins to someone who is my equal and think they can forgive my sins?" As soon as I walked into the church all the statues of Mary and the saints were thrown at me. The Mass was all about the saints, Mary, and repeating the Last Supper every Mass. None of that would save anyone. I felt guilty praying to Mary and the saints. To me it just felt wrong because they are all just people.

The first day that I got home from being in the hospital I knew the Catholic church was wrong. I can feel the disgust that God has for the Catholic Church. I didn't know why at the time; I just knew it was wrong. I told myself that I could never go to a Catholic church again and that made me feel better. I had rosary beads hung up in my room and pictures of Mary hung up in my room, and I would look at them and just feel that same disgust towards them as God does. I had to take everything down in my room that was related to the Catholic religion. It is not that God has anything against Mary, the mother of Jesus or any of the saints. It is not a disgust towards them, it is a disgust of hanging them up, the statues, and praying to them. The problem is that God is a very jealous God. In the Bible there is not any mention of worshipping, praying to, or kneeling to anyone, except to God himself. God is huge, powerful, omnipresent, is the creator of everything, and does not want us praying to anyone else.

I could never understand the Bible when I read it. The Catholic Church never explained the Trinity to me. I also did not understand much about Jesus Christ even after all the years that I went to catechism. I picked up a Bible and I wanted to read all of it. As I started to read the Bible after the cardiac arrest, every word made sense to me. After the second time I read all of it, I could understand the knowledge and the feelings that God gave me. Every word in every verse is very powerful and has meaning to all of it. It is very easy for me to explain through God's Word why the Catholic religion is a false religion.

Idolatry

The Catholic religion puts Mary, the mother of Jesus, almost at the same level as Jesus himself. They encourage you to pray to her. They created the rosary so you can worship Mary. The Catholic Church promotes all of this but, if you listen to the words of Jesus, he immediately lets everyone know that she is not worthy of worship in several ways.

Luke 11:27–28

27: As he said these things, a woman in the crowd raised her voice and said to him, "Blessed is the womb that bore you, and the breast at which you nursed!"
28: But he said, "Blessed **rather** are those who hear the word of God and keep it."

John: 4:23

23: But the hour is coming, and is now here, when the true worshipers will worship the Father in spirit and truth, for the Father is seeking such people to worship Him.

Leviticus: 26:1

1: "You shall not make idols for yourselves or erect an image or pillar, and you shall not set up a figured stone in your land to bow down to it, for I am the LORD your God.

God's words tell us not to put up idols (of Mary or saints) for ourselves. We are to worship the Father in spirit and truth. That was the perfect opportunity for Jesus to open the door to praying or worshipping Mary. Instead, Jesus said blessed rather are those who hear the Word of God and keep it. I keep saying that God's Word is very strong.

Exodus 20:4–5

4: "You shall not make for yourself a carved image, or any likeness of **anything that is in heaven above, or that is in the earth beneath, or that is in the water under the earth,**
5: You shall not bow down to them or serve them for I the LORD your God am a jealous God,

Matthew 4:9–10

9: And he said to him, "All these I will give you, if you will fall down and worship me."
10: Then Jesus said to him, "Be gone. Satan!" For it is written, "**You shall worship the Lord your God and him only shall you serve.**"

Mark 3:32–35

32: And a crowd was sitting around him, and they said to him, "Your mother and your brothers are outside, seeking you."
33: And he answered them, "Who are my mother and my brothers?"
34: And looking about at those who sat around him, he said, "Here are my mother and my brothers!
35: For whoever does the will of God, he is my brother and sister and mother."

There are many verses in the Bible that talk about idolatry and how much God hates it. If you are born of the spirit, the Holy Spirit would be making you feel guilty for kneeling, worshipping, or praying to anyone but God. When you're brought up in the Catholic religion all of this becomes normal for you, and you just need to take the time and read the Bible with an open heart and open mind, and you will also see the amount of idolatry that is involved with the Catholic religion. I cannot find one verse in the Bible where it states to pray to any saints or to Mary, the mother of Jesus. Everything in the Bible says the total opposite: Do not do these things for they are forbidden, and God does not like it. From what I can feel from God is a true disgust of the Catholic religion because of this and several other things that we are going to go over. Mary, the mother of Jesus, cannot save you. There is not any verse in the Bible that says to pray to anyone but God. If you are, you're serving a different god, a false god, that cannot save you.

With the way the Catholic church is set up with statues, pictures, and painted glass of some of the saints and Mary, they are forcing you to sin at every Mass. During the Mass, you kneel several times. Every time you kneel, you worship everything that is in that church. Even the giving out of the Eucharist every Mass, they are basically saying your sins for that week are gone. It doesn't work that way and that is a form of idolatry. At the end of the Mass, everyone shakes the priest's hand, and many say, "Thank you, father." So, there are multiple sins being committed during every Mass, but the worst is the idolatry. I simply cannot say it enough. God really does not like that. He tells us throughout the Bible. God was very angry with the golden calf. This is not my opinion. Everything in this book is directly from God himself.

Ultimate Authority

As a Christian, my ultimate authority is God's Word. God talks to me when I read the Bible. When I read the Bible, the quotes from Jesus are Jesus talking to me, at least that's what happens to me. When I read it, God talks to me and interprets what he means in his verses. That is not the case in the Catholic religion. God does not interpret things in the Catholic religion, the Church does. A group of people do not have the right to interpret verses for millions of people and make it "law." Such as if you don't believe in purgatory, you're going to hell. That's a good example because there is no purgatory. There are certain things that make me feel a certain way and this is one of them. For God not to be the ultimate authority is a slap in the face for God. This is why I must let everyone know how God feels about certain things he revealed to me. The Roman Catholic Church and they're infallible interpretation of the Bible is what Catholics must believe. They also supplement scripture with traditions, and all this must never be questioned. So, basically, what this means is that if you interpret the Bible in a different way then you're going against the Catholic religion. God doesn't understand how a group of people can interpret what he has said, and then they put their own feelings and thoughts into the verse and interpret it their way then make it look like that is what God has said. At the end of the day, the Catholic Church is just a business looking to make a lot of money off what God has said.

Revelation 22:18–19

18: I warn everyone who hears the words of the prophecy of this book: if anyone adds to them, God will add to him the plagues described in this book,
19: and if anyone takes away from the words of the book of this prophecy, God will take away his share in the tree of life and in the holy city, which are described in this book.

Another issue with the Catholic Church that God does not like is how the priests are called "father." It is throughout the church where they call the bishop's and the priests "father."

Matthew 23:9

9: And call no man your father on earth, for you have one Father, who is in heaven.

My question is this: "If we see a clear verse in the Bible that clearly states to call no man 'father,' why does the Catholic Church promote calling bishops and priests father?" It is written in black and white and it's a very simple verse but everyone just brushed it aside and thinks things like this just don't matter. It does matter because it is in the Bible and we are supposed to believe these words in the Bible are from God, but the Catholic Church disregards a simple verse and makes up their own version of the Bible. It is things like this that angers God. God hates sin; every time someone calls a priest "father" they are committing a sin. The Bible cannot contradict itself. Jesus even says honor thy father and mother. If you have the Holy Spirit inside you guiding you, it is easy to see the difference between the father of a child and someone who is teaching the Word of God. You would understand the difference. The Bible is not contradicting itself. It is actually proving itself as some people are in Christ and have the Holy Spirit and some don't because the Holy Spirit tells you. That is what the Holy Spirit is for.

Purgatory

The Catholic religion teaches you that there is this place called "purgatory." This is a belief that after you die, and you love God but die in an imperfect moral and spiritual state, you can still be perfected after you die in purgatory. God said that the Bible does not contradict itself; so, I can give you one verse that makes the possibility of someone going to purgatory after death impossible.

Romans8:1–2

1: There is therefore no condemnation for those who are in Christ Jesus.
2: For the law of the Spirit of life has set you free in Christ Jesus from the law of sin and death.

When Jesus was on the cross right before he gave his spirit he said, "It is finished."So those that are saved by Jesus Christ have no punishment after death. It would be a contradiction if after you die you must go somewhere else to suffer if you are saved. When Jesus died on the cross, he took the wrath of God the Father for all our sins so that we did not have to. If you must go somewhere else after you die to suffer, that is disrespecting Jesus and what he did for all of us. The Catholic religion wants to come along and say Jesus did not die for all our sins, only some of them. The sad thing is that the Catholic Church is teaching that if they do not believe in purgatory that you will go to hell. Think about this if Jesus was in front of you right now. Would you tell him that he was not enough to get you into heaven? The Creator of everything and all of us was not good enough to get you into heaven. If you are Catholic and you are part of that religion that is what you have to say to Jesus when you see him. If you really think and believe in something like that, you should pray to God for guidance. You cannot pick and choose what you do believe in and what you do not believe in. This is the case for any religion. You must believe in all of it or none of it. Especially if you are involved with that church and you're going to Mass on a regular basis. You're supporting what their beliefs are. I do not like to label myself as anything. My religion is Jesus Christ. I'm not going to put a label on myself that I do not believe in 100 percent.

Technically, if you have to go to purgatory before you can go to heaven that would be a work that we did. That would be another contradiction in the Bible.

Ephesians 2:8–9

8: For by grace you have been saved through faith. And this is not your own doing; it is the gift of God,
9: not a result of works, so that no one may boast.

I urge all of you to sit down and read the Bible. Do not go by my words or anybody else's words, except for any word that comes out of God's mouth. I also urge you to pray to God for guidance and help to understand his word. This whole section is very important. Once you see the truth you will realize the Catholic religion cannot save anyone. God can save whomever he chooses. But if you're following this religion, like many others do, you really do not know God. The feeling that I get from God is that many people think they are saved, but they are not. They go to church every week and pray at night, but they are walking into a place where people pray to idols, which God hates, believing in things that are contradicting the Bible and do not truly know God. God's Word is very powerful, you really do not know how powerful his words really are. If you don't understand a verse, keep praying to God until you understand it. God wants me to remind you of a very powerful verse in the Bible.

Matthew 7:21–23

21: "Not everyone who says to me, 'Lord, Lord,' will enter the kingdom of heaven, but the one who does the will of my Father who is in heaven.

22: On that day many will say to me, 'Lord, Lord, did we not prophesy in your name, and cast out demons in your name, and do many mighty works in your name?'
23: And then will I declare to them, 'I never knew you; depart from me, you workers of lawlessness.'

Matthew 7:13–14

13: "Enter by the narrow gate. For the gate is wide and the way is easy that leads to destruction, and those who enter by it are many.
14: For the gate is narrow and the way is hard that leads to life, and those who find it are few.

My fear is that a lot of people are going to read that and say, "No, that's definitely not me." Jesus is talking about the murderers, and the rapist, and the thieves; basically, he is just talking about bad people. The problem with looking at it like that is that we are all enemies of God until we are saved, and the Holy Spirit enters us. God hates all sin. Having a bad thought in your head is the same as doing it in God's eyes. There is about 1.2 billion Roman Catholics in the world right now. That does not sound like a narrow gate to me. To me, that gate is wide, and the way is easy. You could be a millionaire and send millions of dollars into churches or to help the people that have no food, that does not mean anything in God's eyes. God wants you to know him and to know his word and to realize that you cannot love this world and God at the same time. Whoever loves this world their father is Satan. This subject really bothers me and brings a lot of pain to me. I know how God feels about the Catholic Church. It will not save you because it teaches you to sin on a regular basis. Every time you pray to Mary or the saints it is angering God. Every time you walk out of a Catholic Mass you have just committed a multitude of sins including worshipping false gods. I honestly get the feeling that

Satan had a hand in developing this and from the shadows runs the Roman Catholic religion. From the knowledge I have from God, that makes the most sense. Let everyone believe that they are doing the right thing, be dedicated to the religion and just not opening your eyes to the truth. When the Jews were praying to the golden calf, God wanted to go down and destroy all of them. You have a billion people praying to false gods, basically making up their own god in their head and they think they are saved. At the end of the day, Satan has people with a veil over their eyes. You need to be baptized by the Holy Spirit in order to receive him and be saved by Jesus. If you think you're doing everything right, you have blinders on and you're not looking for the truth. You need to find out the truth through God. You're obviously not reading the Bible or understanding it. If you understood it, you would not be praying to people. You need to find Jesus.

God can save whoever he wants. But if you are praying and worshipping people, if you think that the blood of Jesus is not enough to save you and you need purgatory, if you think the Eucharist wipes out your sins for the week, or if you have not been baptized by the Holy Spirit, which is totally different from water baptism as a baby, then you must repent and get to know Jesus Christ. I pray that God opens your eyes to the truth. I cannot say that a Catholic will not be saved. I am just showing you all the sins you are committing on a regular basis. Jesus did not teach any of these things, in all reality you are creating your own god. You are going against the Word of the only living true God. It really opens the door to the possibility that you will not be saved. Do not listen to me. I urge you to find in the Bible where it tells us we need to pray the rosary, to Mary and all the saints. If you can find it in God's Word, then do it. Do not let a church, priest, tradition, a family member, or anything else decide your faith. Let God and God's Word direct you.

Mormonism

This religion is based and started by someone that is a false prophet. That should be a huge red flag but that isn't even the worst of it. I am very sorry if what I say sounds rude or inappropriate. I just do not understand how anyone could follow this religion. I will explain why I feel like this: President Smith then stated that the meeting had been called, because God had commanded it; and it was made known to him by vision and by the Holy Spirit. It was the will of God that they should be ordained to the ministry and go forth to prune the vineyard for the last time, for the coming of the Lord, which was nigh - even fifty-six years should wind up the scene. This prophecy was spoken by Joseph Smith in 1835 and recorded by Oliver Cowdery. The fifty-six years were passed by 1891. (IRR.org) This one of many false prophesies. All it takes is one wrong prophecy to prove you are lying and deceiving. God is never wrong.

Matthew 7:15

15: Beware of false prophets, who come to you in sheep's clothing but inwardly are ravenous wolves.

Deuteronomy 18:20–22

20: But the prophet who presumes to speak a word in my name that I have not commanded him to speak, or who speaks in the name of other gods, that same prophet shall die.'
21: And if you say in your heart, 'How may we know the word that the LORD has not spoken?
22: when a prophet speaks in the name of the LORD, if the word does not come to pass or come true, there is a word that the LORD has not

spoken; the prophet has spoken it presumptuously. You need not be afraid of him.

I included all of that so you can see that God says if someone claims to be a prophet of God, and the word does not come to pass, this is a false prophet. God is never wrong. If you look up the prophecies of Joseph Smith, the founder of Mormonism, he was wrong numerous times and, according to God, if you're wrong once then you are not a prophet of God. This person founded a new religion, introduced new doctrines, and revised the Bible. There are just too many inconsistencies. Polygamy, eternal progression, and many other things that Joseph Smith made up are taught in their religion. The thing that bothers God the most is Mormonism claims that our Lord Jesus Christ and Satan are brothers . . . is there anything else that needs to be said? He also does not like that Mormonism said he was "born." From the beginning it's been the Father, the Son, and the Holy Spirit. Anything that teaches anything else is false and is a slap in the face of our Lord and Savior. That is one of the biggest insults to God. If you cannot see that, you do not know God.

Revelation 22:18–19

18: I warn everyone who hears the words of the prophecy of this book: if anyone adds to them, God will add to him the plagues described in this book,
19: and if anyone takes away from the words of the book of this prophecy, God will take away his share in the tree of life and in the holy city, which are described in this book.

Making a statement that our Lord and Savior Jesus Christ is Satan's brother, is something that has been added. Everyone has been warned about this. Mormonism also teaches that there are many gods.

Isaiah 43:10–12

10: "You are my witnesses," declares the LORD, "and my servant whom I have chosen, that you may know and believe me and understand that I am he. Before me no god was formed, nor shall there be any after me.
11: I, I am the LORD, and besides me there is no savior.
12: I declared and saved and proclaimed, when there was no strange god among you; and you are my witnesses," declares the LORD, and I am God.

Once you hear that any religion has the existence of many gods, that is a false religion. Jesus does not understand how anyone could believe that Satan is his brother, and there are multiple gods. We must accept that some people are going to hell. That is between God and them. All we can do is continue to learn and aspire to be like Jesus Christ. It amazes me that someone, over a thousand years later, completely changed the Bible and people believe it. If you truly know Jesus, the Holy Spirit will never allow you to believe that Satan and Jesus are brothers. The Bible is also changed. This was obviously Satan going to Joseph Smith, just as he went to Adam and Eve.

Deuteronomy 4:39–40

39: know therefore today, and lay it in your heart, that the LORD is God in heaven above and on the earth beneath; there is no other.
40: Therefore you shall keep his statutes and his commandments, which I command you today, that it may go well with you and with

your children after you, and that you may prolong your days in the land if the LORD your God is giving you for all time."

Something really sticks out from this verse. You have a choice of what you choose to believe. If you read any other Bible, not from Joseph Smith, it tells you exactly what God said. He is the only God. Just remember you're not just going against the Word of God yourself, you are also teaching a false religion to your children. I just do not understand why you cannot look at a regular Bible, read it, and see everything that was added by one person. That is sad that you believe one person, instead of forty people over 1,400 years, all saying the same thing. You choose the one that is a proven false prophet.

Everyone thinks Satan has horns and is red and looks evil. That is the total opposite of how he looks. He was a high-ranking angel. So, he can show up with the bright white light, have the wings and outfit of one of God's angels. He also has a third of all the angels with him. These angels are obviously finding vulnerable people and then that person thinks he had one of God's angels talk to them. If you are a saved Christian, they cannot bother you. Jesus destroyed all enemies for us and protects us, even with all that. If I ever saw an angel, I would be making sure they are a servant of Jesus Christ. Plus, the Holy Spirit would tell me. If anyone does not put Jesus Christ first as my God, then it is useless to me. It just amazes me that Mormons fall for this trick. If you're not saved by Jesus, you will not hear his voice.

Many Mormons say that they just got this "feeling" when they heard about it. They believe that it was from God. Our hearts and feelings can be very deceitful. You cannot trust that. Your heart tells you, "Just one more beer," and then I will stop. Our hearts tell us, "Well, if this person isn't in my life everything would be perfect." Do you know how many murderers think like that? A lot. Always go by the Word of God, and do not use a Mormon Bible. It has been changed to back up what Joseph Smith taught. The true Word of God explains everything correctly. The Father, the Son, and the Holy Spirit have been there from the beginning. Do not trust your heart, trust God.

The sad thing is that Jesus went through much more than anyone can comprehend. He was crushed by the Father so that everyone could go to heaven.

Judaism

For this topic I am going to tread very lightly. Jewish people have always been God's chosen people. As far as this religion goes, they only use the Old Testament. They believe Jesus was a mighty prophet, but not the savior. They do not believe Jesus is God. It's as if God views them as stubborn and set in their ways. But, in time, they will be able to see the truth. I just hope and pray that it will be sooner rather than later. In the end, everyone will bow down and confess that Jesus is the savior for the whole world and is God. The sad thing is that Jesus is mentioned throughout the Old Testament. I will give you verses from the Old Testament and challenge you to hear and understand the Word of God; and, if they're not talking about Jesus, who are they speaking of in these verses? In chapter 8 of the book of Daniel, there are many references to Jesus Christ.

The Son of Man Is Given Dominion

Daniel 7:13–14

13: I saw in the night visions, and behold, with the clouds of heaven there came one like a Son of Man. And he came to the Ancient of Days and was presented before him.
14: And to him was given dominion and glory and a kingdom, that all peoples, nations, and languages should serve him; his dominion is

an everlasting dominion, which shall not pass away, and his kingdom one that shall not be destroyed.

It is truly amazing that Daniel was thrown into the lion's den with the lions and the lions never went near him. Angels were present and kept the lions away from Daniel. That is the power of our God. After that happens, Daniel has many dreams, they were interpreted, and all had to do with Jesus Christ taking over the world.

Psalm22:16–18

16: For dogs encompass me; a company of evildoers encircles me; they pierced my hands and feet—
17: I can count all my bones—they stare and gloat over me;
18: they divide my garments among them, and for my clothing they cast lots.

Zechariah12:10

10: And I will pour out on the house of David and the inhabitants of Jerusalem a spirit of grace and pleas for mercy, so that, when they look on me, on him whom they have pierced, they shall mourn for him, as one mourns for an only child, and weep bitterly over him, as one weeps over a firstborn.

This points out exactly what happened when our Lord and Savior Jesus Christ was crucified. The Old Testament clearly prophesied the crucifixion of Jesus, but there is more the Old Testament tells us.

Isaiah53:5–12

5: But he was pierced for our transgressions; he was crushed for our iniquities; upon him what's the chastisement that brought us peace, and with his wounds we are healed.

6: All we like sheep have gone astray; we have turned—every one—to his own way; and the LORD has laid on him the iniquity of us all.

7: He was oppressed, and he was afflicted, yet he opened not his mouth; like a lamb that is led to the slaughter, and like a sheep that before its shearers is silent, so he opened not his mouth.

8: By oppression and judgment he was taken away; and as for his generation, who considered that he was cut off out of the land of the living, stricken for the transgression of my people?

9: And they made his grave with the wicked and with a rich man in his death, although he had done no violence, and there was no deceit in his mouth.

10: Yet it was the will of the LORD to crush him; he has put him to grief; when his soul makes an offering for guilt, he shall see his off-spring; he shall prolong his days; the will of the LORD shall prosper in his hand.

11: Out of the anguish of his soul he shall see and be satisfied; by his knowledge show the righteous one, my servant, make many to be ac-counted righteous, and he shall bear their iniquities.

12: Therefore I will divide him a portion with the many, and he shall divide the spoil with the strong, because he poured out his soul to death and was numbered with the transgressors; yet he bore the sin of many, and makes intercession for their transgressors.

Now, please take a moment to let that sink in. I just keep saying how powerful God's Word really is. This describes Jesus without any doubt. It's in the Old Testament. Why is it so powerful? It was the will of the Lord to crush him, you can write a book on that alone. Jesus went through that willingly. Jesus knew what was going to happen. Now you might understand why Jesus was praying so hard in the garden before they took him. This had to happen. If it didn't happen, nobody could stand before God the Father. You really have to read this over and over. There are so many verses that point to Jesus Christ. If you do not see it, this is your Bible, keep praying to God that you see it. This is why the road is so narrow. Everyone believes that God is just going to forgive everyone, and everybody is going to heaven. It's only a select few that hear Jesus, know Jesus, and trust him with everything, and believe they are going to be with him when they die. Honestly, I do not care about going to heaven. I just want to be with Jesus, the Father, and the Holy Spirit. I want to be wherever they are. I think about that a lot. I'd love to see all of my family in heaven but, honestly, I care more about being with Jesus. If my family members go to heaven or hell, it's not my business that is between them and God. I love Jesus above all. I can easily say that because I died, and I felt his love. I pray for God to have mercy on people I know that died. Trust me, that love is all you will ever need. I'm a servant for Jesus. Whatever he wants me to do, I will do it. I know he wants this book done, there are people that God wants them to read it. People need to realize that it's not about a category or a religion, it is all about God. The Father, the Son, and the Holy Spirit. It's about reading his words, seeing his words, feeling his words, and living by his word. I've read several different versions of the Bible. I understand his words in all of them.

I really want Jewish people to find Jesus. I want Catholics, Buddhists, Muslims, and even Christians that really do not know Jesus to know him. Certain religions just do not teach about Jesus. I was Catholic and did not know Jesus. I just see Jesus all over the Old Testament and that's what I'm trying to show you.

Micah 5:2–4

2: But you, O Bethlehem Ephrathah, who are too little to be among the clans of Judah, from you shall come forth for me one who is to be ruler in Israel, whose coming forth is from of old, from ancient days.
3: Therefore he shall give them up until the time when she who is in labor has given birth; then the rest of his brothers shall return to the people of Israel.
4: And he shall stand and shepherd his flock in the strength of the LORD, in the majesty of the name of the LORD his God. And they shall dwell secure, for now he shall be great to the ends of the earth.

This next verse really stood out for me. It shows that Jesus was there from the very beginning. God did not waste any time letting us all know that God has three Divine Persons. It shows that the Father was never alone, even from the very beginning. I feel that God was making it known that it's not just the Father. The Father is trying to show in a very subtle way that he just did not create things, he created everything through his Son. God really wants this point to be shown. I get the feeling that this should have been highlighted so that throughout the Old Testament the Father lets us know that he is not God alone but God is the Father and the Son and the Holy Spirit.

Genesis 1:26

1: Then God said, "Let us make man in our image, after our likeness. And let them have dominion over the fish of the sea and over the birds of the heavens and over the livestock and over all the earth and over every creeping thing that creeps on the earth."

So, if God was by himself from the very beginning, who is God talking about when he says, "let us," "in our image," and "after our likeness"? The Father made everything through Jesus his Son. In the very first chapter of God's Word, the Bible lets everyone know that Jesus was there with him. The Father just doesn't spell it out perfectly, it's the same way in the whole Bible. Everything prophesied in the Old Testament came true and it was the same with the New Testament. The Father tells us everything about his Son. He tells the who, what, why, and even where and when. You just have to pray to God, then read these verses with an open mind and heart. I understand the push back. I would not entertain anything that did not involve Jesus. I understand it is different for me because I was in the presence of Jesus, and he did talk to me. Jesus did this for a reason. There are other people that Jesus has spoken to. I'm definitely not the only one, there are many. All you have to do is look at things and read things with an open heart. The Jewish people were always God's people. That is obvious throughout the Old Testament. It is also obvious that the Father spoke about his Son in detail so that everyone would know when he was coming. Once Jesus came, he brought the Holy Spirit. The Holy Spirit guides us and points us to the Father and the Son. You're hearing from the Holy Spirit right now. I'm just a tool that God is using to do his will. These words are from the Holy Spirit. The Holy Spirit is guiding me to what message that God wants to send out. As I previously mentioned, after I read the Bible a few times there were certain verses that just stuck out to me and I wrote them down. Most of those verses are the ones that I am using in this book. The Holy Spirit guides those who are saved. That is how we know that the Bible is God's Word. The Holy Spirit was guiding everyone that wrote the Bible and that's why we can be confident that God's Word is true. That is also why the Bible cannot contradict itself. The Old Testament prophesied the powerful fact that our Lord and Savior Jesus Christ was coming. Without Jesus Christ none of us can be in the presence of God. We are truly blessed that God allowed a way for us to be saved, by his wounds we are healed. Our wonderful God is one being with three Persons: the Father, the Son, and the Holy Spirit. Please open your heart and mind, pray for understanding, then read the Bible and you will see that there is only one way to the Father. The biggest problem with the Jewish people is perception. They were expecting a mighty king with a mighty army, not someone coming into Jerusalem on a donkey. The mighty King of Kings, the true son of God, is coming in with great power and glory. The one difference is that this will be the second coming of Jesus Christ. The only problem is you must believe that he already came once. That is the Jesus Christ you must believe that is coming back.

I have a vision of Jesus Christ on Mount Sinai being worshiped by all Jewish people. They will all recognize him as their Lord and Savior.

John 6:35

35: Jesus said to them, "I am the bread of life; whoever comes to me shall not hunger, and whoever believes in me shall never thirst.

John 14:6

6: Jesus said to him, "I am the way, and the truth, and the life. No one comes to the Father except through me.

Islam

Islam originated from several other religions. Islamic prophet Muhammad was born in Mecca at approximately AD 570. So, this was 500 years since Christianity started. The story is basically Muhammad started receiving divine revelation when he was forty years old from the angel Gabriel. This would later form the Koran. The Koran was completed about 500 years later (than the Bible) around 650AD {www.Quora.com) This was after the death of Muhammad. There was some questioning if this was a religion or just something for political reasons. In their religion Jesus is not God. He is just a prophet. The Bible warned about this, with both Islam and later Mormonism. It is very easily explainable. Satan himself or one of his angels visited Muhammad to influence these people into starting a new false religion.

2 John 1:9–11

9: Everyone goes on ahead and does not abide in the teachings of Christ, does not have God. Whoever abides in the teaching has both the Father and the Son.

10: If anyone comes to you and does not bring this teaching, do not receive him into your house or give him any greeting.

11: for whoever greets him takes part in his wicked works

1 John 4:1–3

1: Beloved, do not believe every spirit, but test the spirits to see whether they are from God, for many false prophets have gone into the world.

2: By this you should know the Spirit of God: every spirit that confesses that Jesus Christ has come in the flesh is from God,

3: **and every spirit that does not confess Jesus is not from God. This is the spirit of the antichrist,** which you heard was coming and now is in the world already.

Scholars have identified several preexisting sources for some Koranic narrative (Wikipedia, "Historical Reliability of the Quran"). The Koran assumes its readers' familiarity with the Christian Bible and there are many parallels between the Bible and the Koran.

There are two major flaws about how the religion even started. As I've mentioned before Satan or one of his angels obviously gave false information to Muhammad. The Bible states that if someone comes to you and does not recognize Jesus Christ as God they are a false prophet. The second major flaw in this religion is that nobody wrote it down for 200 years. It was 200–300 years before anyone wrote anything about this religion. If I take one book in the Bible, I will simply use the book of Matthew as an example and say that this was a prophecy given to me by an angel. How accurate would my story be if I did not write it down? I am not talking about a sentence or paragraph. It is an entire book. Then multiply that by 200 years. It is humanly impossible to retain that much information in your head with multiple people over hundreds of years. Just by the Koran teaching that Jesus Christ is not God makes it a false religion. I don't have to go any further than that. I just wanted to give you multiple examples of why Islam is a false religion.

I just wanted to explain the most popular religions. I know that there are many more out there and you can easily find why a religion is false. If you noticed, a few of them were started by people that said that they saw an angel. None of them saw God the Father or Jesus Christ, in fact they put Jesus Christ as not being God. It is amazing how many times that Jesus warns us about false prophets. Christianity is the only religion where God entered his own creation to absorb everyone's sins. All the others bring men into it, giving us a role in our own salvation. That is not the way it works. Our righteousness and our forgiveness of sins all come from God. We have no role in that process. It is a gift from God. For some people, they have to feel like they did something, anything, for their salvation. They cannot accept they played no role at all. Their salvation is a gift from God. We did not do anything to attain our salvation.

There is a limit for me to dissect these religions because it is so obvious as to why they are false religions. With Islam I find it very difficult to believe that something by word of mouth could be accurate for 200 years.

I remember something that they did in middle school where the teacher told somebody a sentence and passed it on, without writing it; by the time it got to the last student, the sentence was completely different. Between that and not recognizing Jesus Christ as God it is immediately false. Going through what I went through, it is impossible for me to even think it has any credibility. Once a religion does not recognize Jesus Christ as God, I will not waste my time to go through a false religion. It is the same thing with Mormonism. Another situation where somebody saw something and made many false prophecies, changed the Bible, and totally disrespected Jesus Christ by putting him in the same sentence as Satan and having "many" gods. I just cannot believe that people would actually believe something so unspeakable. I would be embarrassed with a statement like that.

I'm sorry. Through my words you can tell that the subject hurts me. If you died, and you met Jesus Christ and felt his love alone, you would understand. I felt his love; he gave me information and gifts to help me explain things. Then, he healed my body and mind and has been with me though the most difficult times in my life. He never abandons me, like everyone else did in my life. He brought me back. He brought me back again, and you know what? He has not asked anything of me, just to love and trust him. No matter how tough things get, Jesus Christ is here, with me, holding me because I am sad right now. He tells the rough waves coming to smash into me, "Peace, be still," and they listen. Then everything is calm again. Everything is fine again. Do not tell me that Jesus is not God.

Just remember that this is God's Word, but God can save anyone. Salvation is between God and that person. I stand by my beliefs and the Bible. I swear I do my best to always not judge anyone. But I am not perfect. Sometimes, I see certain terrible crimes on TV and I say to myself, "That is clearly evil." I repent to Jesus when I have any thoughts or feelings that are not biblical. I do not repent for every sin; I have a bad memory sometimes. We are all human; we all make mistakes and we all sin. That is why we all must repent.

CHAPTER 5

INTERPRETING THE BIBLE

The first thing that you have to do is to look at the Bible as a whole. It all blends together. Every paragraph, verse, and word have a meaning for it. Everything from Genesis to Revelation will not contradict itself. God's Word is one of the most powerful things in the world. The only thing that is stronger is God himself. I always hear questions about how can so many people write the Bible and all of it is from God. The truth is very easy, the Holy Spirit wrote the Bible. When you are one of God's children the Holy Spirit dwells within you. If you are baptized by the Holy Spirit, you easily understand that. It is difficult to completely understand without it. The Holy Spirit is part of God, it is God's Spirit. The Trinity is made up of one being that has three Persons. The Trinity is God the Father, Jesus Christ, his only Son, and the Holy Spirit. It must be noted here that all three Persons have always been and always will be. It will be awesome to see the Father, the Son, and the Holy Spirit on their Thrones in heaven and then watch them combine into one. If the Father is drawing you in, you should be trying to learn about him. That is why I bring in so many verses from the Bible into this book. You must remember there are around 757,000 words in the English Standard Version Bible. It takes time to read the entire Bible. If you truly love God, God is expecting you to read the whole thing.

So, reading the whole thing is the first step, along with finding a Christian church. A Catholic church is not Christian. The next step is when you read the Bible, there are a lot of parables. God wants you to actually think about what you are reading. A lot of it is not just in black and white. There are parables and references to cosmic disturbances. Most of this is not literal. It was God's way of describing things. It was not literal in the Old Testament nor is it literal in the New Testament.

Ezekiel 32:6–7

6: I will drench the land even to the mountains with your flowing blood, and the ravines will be full of you.
7: When I blot you out, I will cover the heavens end make their stars dark; I will cover the sun with a cloud, and the moon shall not give its light.

Psalm 97:2–5

2: Clouds and thick darkness are all around him; righteousness and justice are the foundation of his throne.
3: Fire goes before him and burns up his adversaries all around.
4: His lightnings light up the world; the earth sees and trembles.
5: The mountains melt like wax before the LORD, before the Lord of all the earth.

Ezekiel 38:22–23

22: With pestilence and bloodshed I will enter into judgment with him, and I will rain upon him and his hordes and the many peoples who are with him torrential rains and hailstones, fire and sulfur.

23: So I will show my greatness and my holiness and make myself known in the eyes of many nations. Then they will know that I am the LORD.

All of these verses are in the Old Testament. This shows you how God explains things. I will give you similar verses that are in the New Testament that people try to make literal.

Revelation 6:12–13

12: When he opened the sixth seal, I looked, and behold, there was a great earthquake, and the sun became black as sackcloth, the full moon became like blood,
13: And the stars of the sky fell to the earth as the fig tree sheds its winter fruit when shaken by a gale.

Revelation 12:3–5

3: And another sign appeared in heaven: behold, a great red dragon with seven heads and ten horns, and on his head seven diadems.
4: His tail swept down a third of the stars of heaven and cast them to the earth. And the dragon stood before the woman who was about to give birth, so that when she bore her child he might devour it.
5: She gave birth to a male child, one who is to rule all the nations with a rod of iron, but her child was caught up to God and his throne,

Revelation 17:1–2

1: Then one of the seven angels who had the seven bowls came and said to me, "Come, I will show you the judgment of the great prostitute who is seated on many waters,

2: with whom the kings of the earth have committed sexual immorality, and with the wine of whose sexual immorality the dwellers on earth have become drunk."

As you can see, you see the same words that God used hundreds of years apart. God never changes and never lies. The reason that you can see the same descriptions hundreds of years apart proves that God never changes. In the New Testament sometimes people try to put what's going on today into things that have already happened almost two thousand years ago or interpret it as literal when it is just a description. That's why when you read the Bible you have to read it with a clear head, no previous thoughts, previous teachings, or even your own view that you may have believed in the past. You can literally make Bible verses mean anything. People try to make verses about presidents, people in power, popes, the list goes on. You cannot put things that are happening in the world today while reading the Bible. You must read it with an open mind, open soul, and let God determine what is real and what is not real. Just pick up the Bible and read it like it is 2,000 years old and you're trying to learn about God. Honestly, that is exactly what it is. Nowhere does it say that something on a specific future date will happen. I will get more into this when I go over the end of the age in the second coming of Jesus Christ.

1 Thessalonians 4:16–17

16: For the Lord himself will descend from heaven with a cry of command, with the voice of an archangel, and with the sound of the trumpet of God. And the dead in Christ will rise first.
17: Then we who are alive, who are left, will be caught up together with them in the clouds to meet with the Lord in the air, and so we will always be with the Lord.

Revived by Jesus Christ

1 Thessalonians 5:11

11: Therefore encourage one another and build one another up, just as you are doing.

God does not say to wait and hide for him to come. He does not say to scare people into believing in him. God says to encourage each other. Those who are in Christ know that someday he will come and all of his people will be with him. We know that God does not want us scaring people into believing in him. He wants us to continue what we are doing, which is to love everyone and teach them about Jesus Christ. We must do what God puts in our hearts. We must love God with all our heart, soul, and mind. We must love everyone.

A lot of misinterpreting the Bible comes from our hearts. We can make any verse mean whatever we want it to mean. We have to read the Bible with an open mind. We cannot have any prejudice or previous beliefs as we read the Bible. We sometimes read a verse already thinking it is for the bad people; not me. Just like a lot of Catholics believe the prayer Hail Mary is from the Bible. There is only one specific prayer in the Bible given to us by Jesus and that is the Our Father. We tend to have things that we were taught previously influence us. I was brought up in the Catholic religion. My father would always be telling us that the Rapture was going to happen. There were certain dates that would come and go. He always believed he was going to be taken in the Rapture. That is a perfect example of how something can consume us and believe it so much we know it's true, even though it's not. Then the person dies and it never happens. That's what this book is about. You have to let all of your old feelings and beliefs go. You have to approach the Bible as God's Word, without influence from anything else. If you are stuck on a verse that's fine. You just think about it, pray to God for understanding, look how it relates to the whole Bible. You also look at the verses around it and the meaning will come to you at some point. Even if someone else gives me the meaning of a verse, I take it into consideration, but do not believe it until God shows it to me.

Other Things to Be Careful of

God cares about what's in your heart. Some people say that there is homosexuality in the Bible and they read these verses and say that God does not have a problem with it. We see certain churches loosen up their view of it. What God views as an abomination, we now encourage. So, social factors can sway our view on verses in the Bible. Satan is controlling the things that are on TV and it is affecting our social behaviors. We have become much more understanding about certain things. Once that gets into your heart, it will affect how you interpret the Bible. You really have to put all of those things aside. If we start thinking how the world thinks, we will get further away from God. God wrote the Bible that way for a reason. He can tell the people that truly believe in him and those that do not. There are over a billion people that think that it's OK to pray to Mary, the saints, and the angels. How can so many people read the Bible and be so far away from the truth? It is simple. They are looking at the Bible through glasses of society, rituals, behaviors, and things that were taught to them their whole life. So, they are followers. They are the big flock that goes along with the majority because it's easier. It's easier to do what over a billion people are doing than to do the truth and go against everyone. That is a perfect example of how the society around you affects your interpretation of the Bible. What does TV promote? What gets the most views? The things with sex, violence, and things we substitute God for. I cannot think of one thing on TV and the majority of what is online that God would approve of. But that is what we do for much of the day. It is so sad. So many people just do not see the truth. Spend some of that time reading the Bible and praying to

God. Peter, one of Jesus' disciples, denied that he knew Jesus three times. He did not see Jesus die and be resurrected yet. That was a scary time because of the people around him and the lack of faith and understanding made him think a certain way. We do the same thing.

Matthew 15:14

14: Let them alone; they are blind guides. And if the blind lead the blind, both will fall into a pit.

Matthew 15:19

19: For out of the heart come evil thoughts, murder, adultery, sexual immorality, theft, false witness, slander.

2 Timothy 2:15

15: Do your best to present yourself to God as one approved, a worker who has no need to be ashamed, rightly handling the word of truth.

It truly is all about what is in your heart. If your heart is pure and you have the Holy Spirit guiding you, you will be fine. Once you're in Christ none of these things will affect you. That is why I had such a hard time reading the Bible before I was saved. Once I was saved, I knew what was right and what was wrong. I did not see any gray areas in anything. I understand I was given a gift, but anyone that is saved will get the correct interpretation. It might take time and prayer, but it will happen. If you keep having a lot of roadblocks, keep praying. There could be something going on that you know you need to get out of your life. If you really want to be saved and cannot figure out why you are not, then you must look at yourself. There may be something that God wants you to pray to him about, to help you overcome it. Do not forget, God is very loving and very forgiving. The blood of Jesus Christ can cleanse anyone at any time. The choice is yours.

Ultimately, the biggest things that affect our interpretation of the Bible is what the world around us is doing. We add to our previous beliefs or traditions and what's in our heart. I was blessed because God took out all my previous false beliefs, cleaned me with the blood of Jesus Christ, and gave me the Holy Spirit. Once you're born again, that is exactly what happens. Along with that God gave me additional information for the purpose of telling everyone the truth.

I really encourage you to join a Bible study group. You will go over different verses. Then you talk about them and, in most cases, you see the true meaning. We cannot look at five verses and conclude without considering the rest of the Bible. That is how a lot of false preachers make their money. They will take a verse or two and make it into something totally different. That is how people can be fooled. You figure it is right from the Bible. A preacher cannot take three verses from different parts of the Bible and try to tell you that killing certain people is right or that it is OK to have multiple wives. People have done that and still do. God speaks against those things multiple times in the Bible. You have to always interpret the Bible as a whole. In situations like that, you will see the Bible contradict itself. That is one thing the Bible will never do. That is how you test anything, by the Word of God.

CHAPTER 6

THE RAPTURE—THE END OF THE AGE

I can tell you that God the Father is looking down and asking, "Why are so many ignoring me? I AM the Lord your GOD!"

I will be going over the Rapture and the end of the age.There are some references to the Second Coming but I fully explain that in the last chapter. Some verses that you might think pertain to the Rapture may in fact be about one of the other two. I am going to talk about the main verses that people use to explain these things. They just might not be in the order you think. You might have to read this chapter a couple of times so the verses make sense. Just to let everyone know, with the exception of the Second Coming, everything in the book of Revelation has already occurred.

Rapture definition:

In an expression or manifestation of ecstasy or passion

A mystical experience in which the spirit is exalted to a knowledge of divine things.

Revelation 1:1

1: The revelation of Jesus Christ, which God gave him to show his servants the things that must **soon** take place. He made it known by sending his angel to his servant John,

How many times *rapture* is mentioned in the Bible: 0
In this section, all I am doing is showing you that the Rapture and the second coming of Christ are not two different things. All of the verses related to Jesus taking all of his followers to heaven is all one thing. As far as tribulations go, the worst tribulation has already happened. You will see that in The End of The Age.

The idea of a *rapture* as it is currently defined is not found in historic Christianity but is a relatively recent doctrine of Evangelical Protestantism. (Wikipedia, "Rapture")

These are some of the main arguments for a rapture. When you read the next three verses and ignore the third verse then you might have an argument. These verses have nothing to do with a rapture, unless you're expecting to disappear into a corpse, this is why we must read the entire Bible. We must use verses before and after to further explain what God is saying.

Luke 17:34–36

34: I tell you, in that night there will be two in one bed. One will be taken and the other left.
35: There will be two women grinding together. One will be taken and the other one left."
36: And they said to him, "Where, Lord"? He said to them, "Where the corpse is, there the vultures will gather."

Many people like to use one verse and ignore the next verse. Then also ignore the same exact words explaining it better in another book. Matthew has the same verses, but he is talking about the second coming of Jesus Christ. The Bible cannot contradict itself.

Matthew 24:37–42

37: For as were the days of Noah, so will be the coming of the Son of Man.

38: For as in those days before the flood they were eating and drinking, marrying and giving in marriage, until the day when Noah entered the Ark,

39: and they were unaware until the flood came and swept them all away, so will be the coming of the Son of Man.

40: Then two men will be in the fields; one will be taken and one left.

41: Two women will be grinding at the mill; one will be taken and one left.

42: Therefore, stay awake, for you do not know on what day your Lord is coming.

So, why would Matthew use the same words to talk about the Second Coming, and Luke calling that same day a rapture? I can tell you now, most of the verses people use for some "rapture" are verses for something totally different. These two examples completely throw out the possibility of a rapture because if God takes anyone, it is the second coming of Jesus Christ.

The knowledge God gave me the ability to end the Rapture debate. Those verses prove, if any of God's people just disappear, it's the Second Coming. This certainly makes a big difference and it shows you what is meant by those verses. It is obviously two different verses from different parts of the Bible.

You cannot have tunnel vision when you're trying to make something up. The Bible can be very confusing and we cannot try to pull verses and make our own little story. There is more.

1 Corinthians 15:50–52

50: I tell you this, brothers: flesh and blood cannot inherit the kingdom of God, nor does the perishable inherit the imperishable.
51: Behold! I tell you a mystery. We shall not all sleep, but we shall all be changed,
52: in a moment, in the twinkling of an eye, at the last trumpet. For the trumpet will sound, and the dead will be raised imperishable, and we shall be changed.

(This happened when Jesus gave up his spirit, during the earthquake, the dead had risen and went into the cities to give the Gospel in their spirit form, then went to heaven. When the second coming of Jesus Christ happens, everyone on earth will immediately go to their spirit state. Today, when you die, you immediately become your spirit and it goes to heaven or hell.)
What all these verses is telling you is that in a twinkling of an eye, the trumpet will sound and everyone will be transformed from a body to a spirit. When you die, you become a spirit in a split second. When I died, I immediately became my spirit while my body was left dead on the floor. Everyone has a spirit. That is how God made us and that is why we are indestructible. The only one who can change that is God himself. It is very different once you become a spirit. You have much more knowledge. It explains everything and it's embedded in you. You know that God is made up of three Persons, the Father, the Son, and the Holy Spirit. It is impossible for you to argue in your head about it. That is why when your body dies, and you become a spirit that every knee shall bow to Jesus Christ as our Lord and confess that

with our mouths. That verse was clearly telling us that when Jesus died and when he comes again, in a split second we will all become spirits (the people that are currently on earth), the same way that it happened after Jesus died.

In the Bible, it says the meek shall inherit the earth. It does not say that all of God's people will go to heaven and all the unsaved people will still be living on this earth. What is happening is that many people are confusing the second coming of Jesus Christ and the Rapture. Once Jesus comes all of his people will be with him and then at the same time God's Great White Judgment shall occur. If God took all of his people to heaven and left all the nonbelievers on earth, what would that accomplish?

Matthew 13:41–43

41: The Son of Man will send his angels, and they will gather out of his kingdom all causes of sin and all law-breakers,
42: and throw them into the fiery furnace. In that place there will be weeping and gnashing of teeth.
43: Then the righteous will shine like the sun in the kingdom of their Father. He who has ears, let them hear.

(This verse is clearly telling us that all the sinners will be sent to hell and God's people will shine.)
With the knowledge that I have gained from Jesus, and I looked into all of these verses, I keep coming to the same conclusion. God does not want us to focus on waiting for a certain day. God wants all of us to repent, believe that Jesus is the only way to heaven, love him with your whole heart and to love others. God does not want people setting dates or sitting around and waiting for something to occur. Enough people have been hurt over this subject. People lost lots of money while the other false preachers made lots of money from

God's Word with misinterpretation. It has also turned a lot of people away from God, because you have pastors that are giving these dates and then nothing happens. People lose hope in the church. That is one of the worst things you can ever do. If you turn someone away from God, you have to repent and pray to God because that is one thing that angers God. As I mentioned before, I can sometimes feel how God feels about something. Idolatry is one thing God hates, but turning someone away from God is up there too. Unless you are a true prophet from God, do not give people false dates of a rapture or second coming. This is why all of us must be ready at any time. The Second Coming is going to happen in a split second and nobody but God knows when that is. God wants us to love each other and help each other. Please just use the Bible and be wary of anyone that is giving certain dates of biblical things happening.

Revelation 1:10–11

10: I was in the Spirit on the Lord's day, and I heard behind me a loud voice like a trumpet

11: saying, "Write what you see in a book and send it to the seven churches, to Ephesus and to Smyrna and to Pergamum and to Thyatira and to Sardis and to Philadelphia and to Laodicea."

(This was the instruction given to John by Jesus Christ, to send each message to the churches.)

Revelation 3:10

10: Because you have kept my word about patient endurance, I will keep you from the hour of trial that is coming on the whole world, to try those who dwell on the earth.

(Jesus wants this message sent to the church of Philadelphia, not to the world at a later date. Jesus was talking to one church. The "hour of trial" was when the Roman Emperor [Nero] gave the order to kill all Christians.)

Here you see a verse that people like to use as an argument for a rapture. What people don't tell you is what comes before that verse. If you just read Revelation 3:10 and tell everyone that there is going to be a rapture, it says it right here, they obviously did not read the verses that came before these. This is why Jesus gave me an ability to interpret verses correctly. Over the last 200–300 years, people have been doing things like this. They're not giving you the verse's correct meaning. All these were letters that were going to be sent to each of the seven churches. It has nothing to do with things that are happening today.

What you must know about the book of Revelation is that the majority of it has already happened. Revelation was written by John while he was locked up in prison for his beliefs in Jesus Christ. During this time, John received multiple visions. Most of them had to do with the end of the age that was coming. For this particular verse I am going to give you the background about it and who it was meant for.

Revelation 1:17–20

17: When I saw him, I fell at his feet as though dead. But he laid his right hand on me, saying, "Fear not, I am the first and the last,

18: and the living one. I died, and behold I am alive forevermore, and I have the keys of Death and Hades.

19: Write therefore the things that you have seen, those that are and those that are to take place after this.

20: As for the mystery of the seven stars that you saw in my right hand, and the seven golden lampstands, the seven stars are the seven angels of the seven churches, and the seven lampstands are the seven churches.

So what does this verse clearly say who it is meant for?

19: Write therefore for the things you have seen, those that are and those that are to take place after this.

Jesus says, "after this," not 2022 or a date thousands of years away.

Some people change it to take a verse like that by itself and present it to people as proof that it is meant for something that it's over 2,000 years later. During that time when Jesus spoke those words, there was a lot going on in the church and people were confused. You had one covenant ending and a new covenant beginning. When someone tells you a single verse like that, it is up to you to go research it and find out the context of the whole chapter and also the whole book, if needed. You also have to keep in mind that it has to flow with the entire Bible. We always want to put ourselves in the Bible, in some way. These prophecies were not meant for us. If you keep thinking like that, you will never see the truth about much in the bible.

The worst tribulation has already occurred. So, if there was a rapture, we are not going to be taken away because something bad is happening on earth. That would be a contradiction in the Bible.

I went over the majority of verses that people have used about a rapture. As you can see, they were used out of context and did not point to anything related to this topic. They're not going to be two separate events happening. There will be one event which is the return of our Lord and Savior Jesus Christ. Christians living on earth should always be prepared for the Second Coming. That will be a beautiful event, one that I pray over and over in my head, but will be nothing like I have envisioned in my head.

The first believers in a rapture started later in church history (Wikipedia, "Predictions and Claims for the Second Coming"). This was not a belief in the early days of Christianity. It is actually a fairly new belief and now a lot of church leaders are prophesying about it even though there is no new information to back it up. It has hurt the church much more than helped it. This led to a lot of false prophets giving dates about when the Second Coming or the Rapture was going to occur. There were different people that gave false dates in: (3) 1914, 1915, 1935, 1943, 1964, 1972, 1975, 1982, 1988, 1994, 2000, 2011, 2013, 2015, 2019, 2020, and 2021. These were all dates given by church leaders. Looks like we have plenty of false prophets to go around. Please stay away from these people. They are not from God. God is never wrong. I do not have respect for anyone that gives dates of a biblical event happening. The Bible tells us that the only one that knows the date of the return of Jesus Christ is God and God alone. Do not try to be God.

All of these things hurt the church. There is nothing good that can come out of putting false dates out there that are not even in the Bible. In most of these cases, people are not going out there spreading the Gospel of Jesus Christ and are waiting for a certain day to come for something that is not going to happen.

God can do whatever he wants. If God wants to bring all of his believers to heaven, then I will be very happy. I told you I did not want to come back when I died. The way that I look at it is It should not matter if there is going to be a rapture, that is God's choice. I look forward to the second coming of Jesus Christ. I know that is definitely going to happen someday. It could happen now or 500 years from now. Even with that, it still does not matter. Anyone can wake up tomorrow and collapse because their heart stopped. I've been through so much and I've seen so many things, things the majority of people have not seen. I've been through things that many people have not gone through.

Basically, people who are hoping for a rapture are giving up on God and want the easy way out. I am not trying to hurt anyone's feelings. If you are hoping and waiting for a rapture, you are waving the white flag. You are telling God that you do not want to fight for God's kingdom. You must look at yourself in the mirror. Do you really love God enough to die for him? I have an advantage. I have felt the love of God. He loves you more than you can comprehend. My blood can never save anyone. But I would give it to help anyone. I would be honored to give my life for my faith. Ask yourself this, "If there is a rapture tomorrow and you go to be with Jesus, what do you do if your child is still here, a spouse, a family member?" Is it going to matter to you?

This Is Not Was Jesus Told Us

Throughout the Bible, Jesus gave us one prayer. Within that prayer is, "Thy will be done, **on earth as it is in heaven.**"If God takes all of his believers off the earth, then the fight is over. The only people left will be the unsaved. You might as well take all Bibles out of the world. It will still be Satan's world, with no opposition. Taking out all of God's people off of the earth really has no purpose if all the unsaved people are left. All of the churches will be empty, there will be nobody to preach the gospel, God will not have any vessels left on earth to save anyone. The Second Coming will not be needed. If God already takes all of his people to heaven, what is the Second Coming for? There will also be a contradiction in the Bible. The meek shall inherit the earth.

This is why a rapture of God's people will not happen; it is not in the Bible. This topic is angering God. It is contributing to what is going to happen. The last chapter explains what is happening.

Matthew 28:19

19: Go therefore and make disciples of all nations, baptizing them in the name of the Father and of the Son and of the Holy Spirit,

The End of the Age

Many people get confused with the end of the age. Some people think that it's the end of the world, or when the second coming of Jesus Christ is and there are a lot of verses that people think are talking about the end of the world. They are really talking about the end of the age. I will go over it so that you'll understand it and you will finally understand a lot of the verses better in Revelation. Before Jesus Christ sacrificed himself, God gave people a way to atone for their sins, but it was all pointing to Jesus. Some of the ways that were used were animal sacrifices and not being able to eat certain things.

Numbers 6:14–17

14: and he shall bring his gift to the LORD, one male lamb a year old without blemish for a burnt offering, and one ewe lamb a year old without blemish as a sin offering, and one ram without blemish as a peace offering,
15: and a basket of unleavened bread, loaves of fine flour mixed with oil, and unleavened wafers smeared with oil, and their grain offering and their drink offerings.
16: And the priest shall bring them before the LORD and offer his sin offering and his burnt offering,
17: and he shall offer the ram as a sacrifice of peace offering to the LORD, with the basket of unleavened bread. The priest shall offer also its grain offering and its drink offering.

The thing that really sticks out of these sin offerings is that God wanted an unblemished lamb as a sin offering every year. The blood of an animal cannot forgive anyone of sin, so what would be the main purpose of doing this year after year? God was preparing them for what was going to happen in the future. God was showing them that the only way to be forgiven was by way of sacrifice. The sacrifice had to be unblemished. A lot of the Old Testament was pointing directly at Jesus Christ. It is different for all of us now, because we know the ending. That was the biggest problem for all of us. It is impossible for any human to be an unblemished, perfect sacrifice for God. Nobody can be in the presence of the Father that is unclean. That is why Jesus said there is no way to the Father but through him.

There is more about sin offerings. This just could not happen anywhere. They had to make a temple for the offerings. There were several different temples, so I will just give you one. They all had to be exact to the specifications that God gave them.

Exodus 26:31–33

31: And you shall make a veil of blue and purple and scarlet yarns and fine twined linen. It shall be made with cherubim skillfully worked into it.

32: And you shall hang it on four pillars of acacia overlaid with gold, with hooks of gold, on four bases of silver.

33: And you shall hang the veil from the clasps, and bring the ark of the testimony in there within the veil. And the veil shall separate for you the Holy Place from the Most Holy.

Revived by Jesus Christ

Exodus: 27:1–3

1: "You shall make the altar of acacia wood, five cubits long and five cubits broad. The altar shall be square, and its height shall be three cubits.

2: And you shall make horns for it on its four corners; its horns shall be of one piece with it, and you shall overlay it with bronze.

3: You shall make pots for it to receive its ashes, and shovels and basins and forks and fire pans. You shall make all its utensils of bronze."

There is more that has to be built, I wanted to give you an idea of how precise God is. They were not making some church for people to go into, they were making a temple that only God and the priest could enter. Do not forget about the curtains. The curtains were what separated God from any human. This is how God's people lived under the Old Covenant. The Holy Spirit was not released to the world yet, so people had to rely on the Ten Commandments and all of these things that were passed down from generation to generation.

Eventually everything changes. The prophecy happens exactly how Jesus said it would happen. There was going to be a very important transition. Just remember if this transition never happened, everybody would go to hell or there was a place in hell, but it was for the righteous. Nobody could go to heaven until the time of Jesus Christ. Up to that point nobody's sins were gone. The only one that could save us is God himself. He chose to lower himself and be born into this world for the sins of everybody. I sit back and think about that a lot. The creator of everyone, and of everything, had to lower himself by being born in this world and be crucified and die for all of us. When I think about that, it just amazes me how much love Jesus and the Father, really has for all of us to do all of this so that we can be in the presence of God. It is very difficult for us to comprehend all of that. The only thing that I can say, with 100 percent certainty, is that

God has a love for us that we can never reciprocate. It is too strong. We have to try and remember how fortunate that our God loves us, calls his sealed ones his children, and never changes. If God had had any feelings like we do, we would all be in grave trouble. God does get mad at us, but every time he does it is because of something we did. Hence, the Flood. Just be grateful that our God loves us, will always be with us and protect us.

Jesus wanted to make sure that everyone knew that the Old Covenant was ending, and the new covenant was starting. A lot of things happened, that is the way Jesus wanted it, so people would believe him.

Luke 23:28–30

28: But turning to them Jesus said, "Daughters of Jerusalem, do not weep for me, but weep for yourselves and for your children.
29: For behold, the days are coming when they will say, 'Blessed are the barren and the wombs that ever bore and breasts that never nursed!'
30: Then they will begin to say to the mountains, 'Fall on us,' and to the hills, 'Cover us.'

(Jesus is telling them to pray for all the Jewish people that were going to be killed when Rome attacks Israel.)

The End of the Old Covenant

Matthew 27:50–52

50: And Jesus cried out again with a loud voice and yielded up his spirit.
51: And behold, the curtain of the temple was torn in two, from top to bottom. And the earth shook, and the rocks were split.

52: The tombs also were opened. And many bodies of the saints who had fallen asleep were raised,

Jesus had to absorb all of our sins, then give up his spirit, for it to become complete, Jesus still had to rise from the dead. Once that happened, the new covenant was going to slowly take over. Once the news was spread and the Holy Spirit started entering more and more people, the new covenant took over. With the earthquake that happened after Jesus gave up his spirit, the curtain was split in two. That signified that there was nothing more between God and man except Jesus Christ. The only way was by the blood of Jesus Christ, forgiveness of all sin, and receiving righteousness through Jesus Christ. This is how the Old Testament and New Testament became all one book. Everything matches up perfectly. Over hundreds of years and around forty different authors, the Bible miraculously is all true, lines up correctly, and all prophecies happened (only God could do that).

At this point, there were many prophecies by Jesus Christ that had to be fulfilled. If these things were not fulfilled, that would make Jesus a false prophet. So, now I will go over the things that Jesus prophesied that would happen as a sign that the new age was now in place.

Luke 21:20–22

20: But when you see Jerusalem surrounded by armies, then know that its desolation has come near.
21: Then let those who are in Judea flee to the mountains, and let those who are inside the city depart, and let not those who are out in the country enter it,
22: for these are days of vengeance, to fulfill all that is written.

In AD 63, the Romans captured Jerusalem. Due to clashes with the Gentiles, the Jewish people revolted in AD 66 and they got all of the Romans out of Jerusalem. At that time, by divine revelation, knowing that Jesus had already told the Christians to escape from Jerusalem, in AD 66, there was a small window of opportunity for all of them to flee Jerusalem. They remembered what Jesus had said about the abomination of desolation. Not one Christian died.

The Abomination of Desolation

Matthew 24:15–18, 21

15: So when you see the abomination of desolation spoken of by the prophet Daniel, standing in the holy place (let the reader understand),
16: then let those who are in Judea flee to the mountains.
17: Let the one who is on the housetop not go down to take what is in his house,
18: and let the one who is in the field not turn back to take his cloak.
21: **For then there will be great tribulation, such as has not been from the beginning of the world until now, no, and never will be.**

(Jesus told them that when you see Judea being surrounded by Roman soldiers to leave immediately. Jesus also says this "great tribulation" will be the worst that the world will ever see, so nothing that bad will happen again, ever.)

One of the reasons that this was the worst tribulation ever was because over a million innocent civilians were killed by Roman soldiers. The Romans were combat-ready soldiers. They killed men, women, and children that had no weapons, were malnourished, and could not fight. The thing that is so disturbing is that they were using swords. It is not like it is today when you can send a missile from miles away. They did not have automatic weapons. They had to walk up to the men, women, and children that did not have any weapons and kill them. I understand they were battle-hardened soldiers, but how can you physically kill an innocent baby? This was a brutal time. The famine, the sickness, and the death before the soldiers got there, then they just wiped everyone out. That is pure evil. That is why Jesus was weeping. That is why Jesus called it the "abomination of desolation."

Unfortunately, just like the crucifixion of Jesus Christ, this had to happen.

The Abomination of Desolation

Matthew 24:15–18, 21

15: So, when you see the **abomination of desolation spoken of by the prophet Daniel,** standing in the holy place (let the reader understand),

Some may bring up the visions of Daniel. He had several visions of this time. That is why the verse says "let the reader understand." It had the same language that was used in the book of Revelation. Daniel prophesied the end of the Old Covenant and the start of the new covenant. This was very important. This told everyone that Jesus Christ was the Son of Man, the Savior of all of God's people.

Daniel 7:27

27: And the kingdom and the dominion and the greatness of the kingdoms under the whole heaven shall be given to the people of the saints of the Most High; his kingdom shall be an everlasting kingdom and all dominions shall serve and obey him.'

Daniel saw many visions about the new covenant starting led by Jesus Christ. In Daniel chapter 8, all these visions were about the different kingdoms that were going to be around at that time. It got to the point where it made Daniel sick for several days. All of it had to do with the worst tribulations that the world had ever seen and nothing like that will ever compare to it. Today, we have many people interpreting these verses as things that are going to happen in the future. That is why I keep saying that the majority of the book of Revelation already happened. The next thing to happen is the second coming of Jesus Christ, with no signs, tribulations, or world-ending events. I pray that everyone is ready for the Second Coming. Whatever chip gets implanted in your hand or forehead has absolutely nothing to do with the mark of some beast. Jesus has already told us he has defeated all our enemies. Please believe the Word of God and not a movie, book, or a pastor that says the end-time tribulations are coming. When Jesus returns, there will not be anything different than what is going on today. He will be like a thief in the night. Just like the times of the Flood. Nobody but God and Noah knew the Flood was coming.

Mark 13:30–31

30: Truly, I say to you, this generation will not pass away until all these things take place.
31: Heaven and earth will pass away, but my words will not pass away.

This verse wraps it up. If you truly believe that all of these verses were not for this time, then you will have to say that Jesus Christ is a false prophet and not God. Jesus says, **"This generation will not pass away until all these things take place." If you believe that Jesus was talking about anything that did not happen during that generation, then you also must believe that Jesus is not the Messiah."** That would mean we are all in big trouble. Jesus prophesied about the end of the age, not the end of the world or the second coming of Jesus Christ. All these verses are talking about the end of the age. The Old Testament sacrifices were being replaced by the New Testament (the crucifixion of Jesus Christ).

After the Romans surrounded Jerusalem and prevented any food or supplies from getting in, this led to famine throughout Jerusalem. There are rumors that some of them tried to rely on cannibalism in order to stay alive. In Jesus' words he warns them that it is going to be a great tribulation, such as has not been from the beginning of the world and never will be. When you hear Jesus prophesied about wars and rumors of wars and famine and great tribulation, just remember he said all those things would happen once Rome decided to wipe out Israel. As Jesus said, all his people, the Christians, would not perish. With nothing able to get in the country, it wore down the whole population. After years of nobody coming in or going out of Jerusalem, it had to be filled with sickness, death, and famine. (2) They massacred most of the remaining population. That is one thing that made me sad. Over a million people were stuck there. The Romans did not allow the noncombatants to leave, nor the women and children. They had no food. Everything was cut off. (2) They did allow some pilgrims to enter the city due to Passover, but did not let them leave.

On April 14th AD 70, the Roman army started besieging Jerusalem. In August of AD 70, Roman forces overwhelmed defenders and set fire to the temple. Approximately 1.1 million noncombatants died in Jerusalem from violence and famine. After the Romans were done, there was virtually nothing left. They were told to kill everyone and destroy what they could . . . . (www.learnreligions.com).

Luke 19:41–44

41: And when he drew near and saw the city, he wept over it.
42: saying, "Would that you, even you, had known on this day the things that make for peace! But now they are hidden from your eyes.

43: For the days will come upon you, when your enemies will set up a barricade around you and surround you and hem you in on every side 44: and tear you down to the ground, you and your children within you. And they will not leave one stone upon another in you, because you did not know the time of your visitation."

1 Corinthians 2:6–8

6: Yet among the mature we do impart wisdom, although it is not a wisdom of this age or of the rulers of this age, who are doomed to pass away.
7: But we impart a secret and hidden wisdom of God, which God decreed before the ages for our glory.
8: None of the rulers of this age understood this, for if they had, they would not have crucified the Lord of glory.

Regarding the second coming of Jesus Christ, and the end of the age there are still a lot of verses in the Bible about them. I feel as though I put the most relevant verses to help explain the topics. It still amazes me that there are so many verses in the Bible written by many different authors over many years and all flows perfectly. We are the ones that change the meaning. We must really look at these verses and try not to use them in a different way. I can understand why people get confused with these verses. Most of the book of Revelation has already happened. But some people try to put these verses as if they are going to happen at a future time. We make it about us. Man has that tendency to make us part of salvation. Jesus was talking about His generation. My view of the Bible is as it is written and when it was written. When I understand that everyone is different, people are going to have different views. The only thing I can do is write down what the Holy Spirit is telling me to write down. Now, I can see the verses as they truly are and understand them. Over the past year, God has helped me a lot to understand the information that he gave me when I died. I'm at a point that, from Genesis to Revelation, everything flows beautifully as one book. One of the biggest things that stand out is that Jesus Christ told them thirty years before it happened. The history books all line up with what Jesus prophesied. It is very difficult to argue that Jesus is not God. Nobody has been that accurate, only God.

People like to take verses like the "abomination of desolation" and use it for the end of the world. As we can see, all those verses talk about the end of the age. I have gone through the entire Bible. I cannot find any verse that talks about any tribulation happening at the end of the world. Jesus tells us that his second coming will be like a thief in the night. We're not going to be in a situation where the whole world is fighting itself and they put chips in our bodies and end all the other ideas that people have come up with.

You would have a point, but Jesus told us something. What he told us means the worst tribulation of the world has already happened.

For then there will be great tribulation, such as has not been **from the beginning of the world until now, no, and never will be.**

During that time, when Nero was in charge of Rome, he had his soldiers looking for Christians to kill them, behead them, or put them on poles around the city, pour gasoline over them, to literally burn them alive. That is where they got the phrase "Roman candlestick." This torture went on for years and years. If you were a Christian at that time, you would have either been beheaded or had a longer painful death if any Roman found out you were Christian. This is why Jesus said that time would be the worst tribulation ever. I have to point this out because many people just do not know of this. In Revelation chapter 13 it talks about the beast with the mortal wound. There they are talking about Nero once again. He sustained a mortal wound but lived. He was working with Satan to kill all Christians. This is why you have to really try to put the pieces together. People make a lot of money from creating events in their mind, but it is not the truth.

I'm not asking all of you to believe my point of view,.I'm asking you to read what God is saying and then you decide. This is the area that causes a lot of confusion. I tried to clear it up the best I could. There are not any verses in the Bible that say something will happen in 2022. It just tells us to be ready for the second coming of Jesus Christ, which I cannot wait for. The thing that really bothers me is how many people are not saved right now! If you are stuck on some rapture, it is not in the Bible. We can agree to disagree. You should not be wasting time on it. The Second Coming is going to happen, and then it is over. Why waste time on stuff like that when there are a lot of people that need to be saved. Put your energy into being a servant of God, not waiting for some star to line up with something or an attack on Israel. The mark of the beast was, once again, talking about something 2,000 years ago. We are not working hard enough. Jesus will ask all of us, "Why are so many people not saved?" Please do not let your answer be, "I was waiting for the Rapture" or "I am trying to figure out who is the 'antichrist'" or "false prophet." None of those matters. Jesus already defeated all of our enemies. We need to fight for souls. That is the true war. All of this other stuff is nonsense. It is done and has been for a long time.

I was talking to God about the Rapture, the end of the age, and the second coming of Jesus Christ. Why has it been such a popular topic? Why did God want it proven that there is no rapture? It just popped into my head. There are two reasons why the second coming of Jesus may be coming sooner than later. Why will all the unsaved get a clear second chance? When God flooded the earth, did he give anyone a warning? If there is a rapture, everyone will figure it out. They will all know and turn to Christ. Did billions of people get that same warning? None of the people that have died over the past 2,000 years got an obvious one-way ticket to heaven. If one-third of the population just disappeared, 80 percent of the people left will become Christians. Nobody else got that same benefit. That is another reason there is no rapture coming, add that to all the other reasons, I'm asking everyone to prepare for the Second Coming. It is scary how many people are not saved. If Jesus came right now, I know how many would be in the sky with Jesus Christ. I cannot tell you the percentage, I am not a prophet. I hope I am wrong.

The Seventh Trumpet

Revelation 11:15

15: Then the seventh angel blew his trumpet, and they were loud voices in heaven, saying, "The kingdom of the world has become the kingdom of our Lord and of his Christ, and he shall reign forever and ever."

It was at this time that our Lord Jesus Christ took his spot next to God the Father. The seven trumpets in the book of Revelation explain everything that happened right before the new covenant began. It was during that time that all the saved people were allowed into heaven. That whole section in Revelation tells how Jesus Christ became the King of all and the Savior of all.

Revelation 11:19

19: Then God's temple in heaven was opened, and the ark of his covenant was seen within his temple. There were flashes of lightning, rumblings, peals of thunder, an earthquake, and heavy hail.

I really do not like to say the same things repeatedly, but everything in the book of Revelation, except for the second coming of Jesus Christ, has already happened. I try to bring in as much of it as I can so you can see the truth. That is also why the surrounding of Jerusalem, which Revelation says for forty-two months, is in Revelation 11:2.

CHAPTER 7

HOW DO I KNOW IF I AM SAVED?

Luke 13:24

24: Strive to enter through the narrow door. For many, I tell you, will seek to enter and will not be able.

This is a question that I hear a lot. The answer varies from person to person. Some tell you that if you just say this prayer, then you are saved. My question to that would be, "Are you God?" Nobody can, or has the right, to tell someone if they say a prayer then they are saved. It is a big question and can have a lot of answers. The ultimate answer is only God truly knows, but there are several signs that God may give you to let you know for sure. Salvation is between God and you. There is nothing else that determines that. I will let you know what the most important thing in your salvation is. What's in your heart and if you know Jesus. There is no specific formula. The Bible tells us that God the Father draws you in, then Jesus saves you and after that the Holy Spirit becomes a part of you to guide you and help you. Some do avoid all that and accept Jesus Christ on their deathbed and God saves them. I would never rely on that one, but it does happen. So how do we know that someone can be saved on their deathbed, right before they die?

Luke 23:42–43

42: And he said, "Jesus, remember me when you come into your kingdom."
43: And he said to him, "Truly, I say to you, today you will be with me in paradise."

This was a criminal next to Jesus at his crucifixion. We do not know much about the thief. We do know that he believed Jesus would be in his kingdom and he also mentioned how Jesus did not do anything wrong. In a few short verses we can see the thief knew he was getting a punishment which he deserved. He also points out that Jesus did nothing wrong. Then he accepts Jesus as God by asking Jesus to think of him when Jesus gets to his kingdom. Then Jesus confirms he is saved and will be with him in paradise.

This tells us that we can be saved at any point up until we die. God has the ability to do whatever he pleases. When you really think about those verses, you can determine that the thief had a good heart and believed that Jesus was the savior. It really comes down to what is in your heart and what you truly believe. If you repent to Jesus, truly believe that Jesus Christ is Lord over your life, that he died on the cross for your sins, and rose from the dead, and sits at the right hand of the Father, then you will be saved. That is what Jesus tells us.

John 3:16

16: "For God so loved the world, that he gave his only Son, that whoever believes in him should not perish but have eternal life."

It's not that easy though. In your heart you have to trust that Jesus, and only Jesus, will save you. There cannot be any doubt in your mind. You must honestly believe, in your heart and mind, that your only way to be saved is through Jesus Christ. Then the Holy Spirit becomes a part of you. You become a completely different creature. Any type of sin bothers you, you might feel the weight of all your past sins. If you truly believe in Jesus (1) you will not want to sin and (2) the Holy Spirit would prevent you from sinning and really make you feel bad about it if you do. When I first got home from the hospital, I could feel a bunch of things that were in my life that were wrong. Anything that I had hanging up in my room that pointed to the Catholic Church was making me sick to my stomach until I brought it down. This is why the magic prayer doesn't work either. If you are truly saved, sin upsets you. You know that all of us are unclean in the eyes of God. God hates sin. A bad thought is enough to send you to hell for eternity, never mind actually willingly committing a sin, you do not have to do anything. We were all born into sin. Not being born by the Holy Spirit, if that never happens, without Jesus you will go to hell for eternity. So that verse sounds easy enough, but when you are saved you are completely changed. Although being saved on your deathbed is possible, I would never encourage anyone to hope for that.

Everyone is different. Normally something happens, it can occur at any time, but for a lot of people, it is at a low point in their life. Something bad happens, it can be pretty much anything. You just reach a low point, and you feel empty, you feel like you have no choices or options. The Bible explains that the Father draws you. God the Father slowly opens your eyes, mind, and heart. God put something into your heart, but you are so used to being a part of this world and it becomes a tug-of-war. You have God pulling you in one direction and the world pulling you into another direction. This tug-of-war can end quickly, or it could go on for years. Satan has programmed us to love this world and everything in it. He preys on your weaknesses and attacks them, making it difficult for you to get away from them. It could be a problem that you're so infatuated with someone or something that you always end up giving in. It could be any sin.

Sex out of marriage, food, idolatry, stealing. It's normally that one thing that you love, and you know you do not want to say goodbye to it and follow Jesus Christ. If you're going to be saved, you reach a point where you do not want to live like that anymore. It is different for everyone, but at some point, you accept Jesus Christ as your Lord and Savior. When this happens you are truly saved, you normally feel very happy, relieved, and you start changing. The Holy Spirit enters you. You finally realize that you need God to give you the strength to overcome everything. It is not you, but God that takes away the feelings of addiction, lust, or whatever you are facing.

At some point you will feel this uncontrollable thirst for God. All you want to do is learn more and more about him. You start reading the Bible and now it makes sense to you. This is a learning phase. If it's a true conversion you will receive the Holy Spirit and that's very important. That's where your thirst for knowledge comes from. It is a huge transition, and everything just looks different to you. You cannot figure out why at first. This is also different for everyone depending on their background. Some people may have read the whole Bible before, and others may have never read it at all. The Holy Spirit is the guide in you as to what you should be focusing on. You definitely feel different though.

Revelation 3:20–22

20: Behold, I stand at the door and knock. If anyone hears my voice and opens the door, I will come in to him and eat with him, and he with me.
21: The one who conquers, I will grant him to sit with me on my throne, as I also conquered and sat down with my Father on his throne.
22: He who has an ear, let him hear what the spirit says to the churches."

So once Jesus saves you then the Holy Spirit teaches you. Jesus is the Bread of Life. It all starts with hearing Jesus, then welcome him into your life. That is the most important step. If you never hear Jesus or know Jesus. Then how can he save you?

Once you're learning and praying it hits you like a ton of bricks. For the first time, you really see yourself as God sees you. You see your sins. The sins you made in the past and the sins that you are doing now. It can be overwhelming. You will just start praying and repenting and you will say to yourself, "Jesus cannot save me with all of these sins." Never doubt the power of Jesus Christ. The only sin that will not be forgiven is to grieve the Holy Spirit. This is when you truly believe that the power of Jesus Christ is from demons, not that he is God. Do not ever do that.

Isaiah 43:25

25: I, I am he who blots out your transgressions for my own sake, and I will not remember your sins.

Hebrews 8:12

12: For I will be merciful toward their inequities, and I will remember their sins no more."

Romans 8:1

1: There is therefore now no condemnation for those who are in Christ Jesus.

Do not let Satan or anyone else get into your head about your sins. Once you are saved by Jesus Christ your sins are wiped out and there is no suffering or purgatory when you die in Christ. That was a difficult experience for me. I saw all my sins. At the end of the day, we have to truly trust God and believe him because he does not lie or change. Every time we question it, we are questioning the Crucifixion. We are questioning the power of Jesus Christ. That is something we should never do.

Then we go through a stage where we look around and want everyone to be saved. You wonder why they can't see it. It's right there in black and white. We cannot forget that this is up to God. God will use us at any time to spread the good news about Jesus. You just can't get frustrated if people do not listen to you. Remember, everyone is conditioned to love the world. The only one who can break through this is God. We can pray for people, spread God's Word, just always remember it is up to God. God is justified either way. If you talk to people about Jesus and they say that you're crazy, God is justified. When Judgment Day comes, God will say I sent one of my servants to talk to you and you did not want to hear it, or you planted a seed that God will use at a later time. That's why I thank God all of the time. Having air for me to breathe is a gift from God. Having a place to live and food to eat is a blessing from God. I am blessed beyond belief because I do not deserve anything. Some people take all of this for granted. People think God owes us something. God does not owe anyone anything. He gave us life and takes care of us; God doesn't have to do that.

Normally, this stage is where you get your calling. Everyone has different gifts to offer. God may put in your heart that you want to be a church leader. He might want you to go spread God's Word in the streets, teach God's Word at a place that does not have any light. Try to convert people from other religions or it could simply be he wants you to work hard at your job and be ready if someone asks you questions about Jesus. I struggled with this for three years. I was not sure which way God wanted me to go or what I should do. I felt as though he brought me back for a specific reason. I had all this knowledge and feelings from God. Then, just a little bit over three years, I finally got my correct diagnosis and found out that I was able to be treated. I knew at that time that I had to write about God and my experiences with him. As soon as I got diagnosed and the episodes stopped, I could just feel what God wanted me to do next. It made sense that it had to be after I got the diagnosis. It would have been difficult for me to write a book if I was still sick and getting episodes. I will tell you not to rush it. Whatever God wants you to do, he will put that desire in your heart. It becomes a burning desire, and it definitely feels like it's something that you need to do. It's always in your head, it will be something that makes you happy doing it, and it will all make sense. You will just keep pushing every day because now you are a new creature. The old you is dead. Now you are alive in Christ. You should see a lot of changes in your life. You'll get the thirst for God, then you will see all your sins and eventually get your calling. It could be anything. The main thing is that you are being molded by God to become more like Christ.

Colossians 3:1–7

1: If then you have been raised with Christ, seek the things that are above, where Christ is, seated at the right hand of God.

2: Set your minds on things that are above, not on the things that are on earth.

3: For you have died, and your life is hidden with Christ in God.

4: When Christ who is your life appears, then you also will appear with him in glory.

5: Put to death therefore what is earthly in you: sexual immorality, impurity, passion, evil desire, and covetousness, which is idolatry.

6: On account of these the wrath of God is coming.

7: In these you too once walked, when you were living in them.

I will caution you to never doubt your conversion. It took 4 years for me to unravel a lot of the information in my head. Sometimes I would ask myself "why am I not fighting evil"? I am still in the same situation. What I did not realize is how much I had learned. I was starting to learn things that are going on in the spirit world. I did not get my big vision until December 2022. That put everything together, taught me more than I could have thought. It allowed me to finish this important book. I also realized how far along I was by being in Christian discussion groups. I could not believe I could answer any question. So please give it time. Jesus does not use our time here. You have to be patient.

2 Corinthians 5:17

17: Therefore, if anyone is in Christ, he is a new creation. The old has passed away; behold, the new has come.

Romans 6:6–8

6: We know that our old self was crucified with him in order that the body of sin might be brought to nothing, so that we would no longer be enslaved to sin.
7: For one who has died has been set free from sin.
8: Now if we have died with Christ, we believe that we will also live with him.

Once we are saved by Jesus, the punishments for our sins were all absorbed by Jesus on the cross. A true conversion will immediately change your life and every day you will become more like Jesus. Once we repent and are saved then God remembers our sin no more. That's why it's important every day to try avoiding sin and repeating the same sins. None of us is perfect, we will still sin, but it should not be at the rate it was before and after you overcome your sin; you should not be doing the same sin over and over. If you struggle with something, talk to a pastor or someone who is in Christ that you trust. Also pray to God to take the urge that causes the same thing to go away. At this point you have the power of Jesus Christ behind you. He defeated all of our enemies, so he definitely can and will help you. You just have to be persistent and keep praying. You try to be as strong as you can, Jesus will do the rest. Sometimes it takes a little while for you to fully trust God with everything. After a little while though you have to get to that point. You have to trust God with absolutely everything in your life. For me, even when something bad happens, I tell God, "I do not understand why this has happened, but I trust you 100 percent no matter what happens." There were several times I was in the hospital before they found out what was causing everything and, at that point, I was very, very peaceful. I knew that it was happening for a reason. I knew that God had his hand in that situation and I knew that no matter what happened that was God's will, even if I died again.(I did get shocked 8–9 times over the two years after, so technically I did die multiple times). Once you trust God with everything in your life everything becomes easier. You no longer have to worry about anything, and you know that God is in control of everything. I'm so much more relieved I just live one day at a time, I try to be the best person that I can be, and I know that God is guiding me to do his will. You have to realize that God literally speaks things into existence. That powerful God that we serve knows what's best for us. He knows what we need before we know, so the best thing for anyone to do is to put everything in God's hands.

False Conversion

There have been many debates about this. It can be a touchy subject. It happens when someone receives God's Word, accepts Jesus

Christ as their Lord and Savior, and everything about them looks like they are saved. Then, after a certain amount of time, something bad happens or they simply walk away from being a Christian. Many people say that this is a false conversion.

Mark 4:16–17

16: And these are the ones sown on rocky ground: the ones who, when they hear the word, immediately receive it with joy.
17: And they have no root in themselves, but endure for a while; then, when tribulation or persecution arises on account of the word, immediately they fall away.

There are no problems with this verse. It is straightforward. These people acting like Jesus is the greatest thing in the universe, but as soon as something happens, they do not trust in God anymore. They are still in love with the world.

John 6:37

37: All that the Father gives to me will come to me, and whoever comes to me I will never cast out.

John 10:26–30

26: but you do not believe because you are not among my sheep.
27: My sheep hear my voice, and I know them, and they follow me.
28: I give them eternal life, and they will never perish, and no one will snatch them out of my hand.
29: My Father, who has given them to me, is greater than all, and no one is able to snatch them out of the Father's hand.
30: I and the Father are one."

These verses are very important. Jesus tells us if we hear the voice of Jesus Christ, then we are saved. What that means is if we understand the gospel of Jesus Christ, that he is the Savior, believe that he died for all of our sins and sits at the right hand of the Father, then you are saved. Once you are saved nobody can come along and take that away from you. You are protected by God the Father and our Lord and Savior Jesus Christ. If you do not understand what the Bible tells us about Jesus Christ, then you have to work on being saved. The way that you do that is by finding a good Christian church, attend all Masses, get in a Bible study group, and spend time with God every day. Take an hour every night to pray to God and read the Bible. If you stay dedicated to that, then the Father is bringing you towards him and his Son Jesus Christ. You cannot do it for a few months and then stop because you do not understand. It takes time, patience, and prayer to be saved by Jesus Christ. What you also have to do is be baptized by the Holy Spirit. After you join a Christian church let them know that you need to be baptized. We cannot get into heaven if we are not baptized by the Holy Spirit. God can do this at any point in your life. I was baptized by the Holy Spirit and born again while I was with Jesus. It was easy to tell once I got home, because I could see all of my sins.

It clearly states that whoever goes to Jesus will be saved and not cast out. It does not say whoever comes to me, and still loves the world, I will not cast out. God knew us before we were born. God knows who is written in the Book of Life and God knows who will be saved and who will not be.

Based on that, these people hear the Word of God and believe that they are saved. The problem is the Father never gave them to Jesus and they did not go to Jesus with 100 percent faith in Jesus. These people still love the world. It may not show right away, but it will show at some point. They are not false converts because they never were in Jesus at any point. Jesus wanted to remind everyone that he knows who he died for and who he did not die for. All the answers are in the Bible. There are people who are constantly trying to fight the Bible, and not accept it or misinterpret it, they just love the world a bit more than they love Jesus. If you think that Jesus would cast a believer out of his hands, then you do not know him. I was given knowledge about God, God also let me in on some of his feelings on certain topics and this is one of them.

Creating Your Own Jesus

The last thing that I'm going to go over in this chapter is that many people create their own Jesus in their head. They will take certain verses out of the Bible that relate to them, and they will live by these verses, but ignore all the other verses. This subject could be in many different chapters of this book, but I chose to talk about it here. Another way that people make up their own Jesus is by saying the Old Testament was the Father and he was mean, and then Jesus came along and just talked about love, loving everybody, being good to people, and everyone is going to heaven. If you read the Bible there are many references to the Old Testament that are in the New Testament. Jesus also mentions hell a lot more than heaven.

Matthew 5:17–18

17: Do not think then I have come to abolish the Law or the Prophets; I have not come to abolish them but to fulfill them.
18: For truly, I say to you, until heaven and earth pass away, not an iota, not a dot, will pass from the Law until all is accomplished.

Revived by Jesus Christ

Matthew 21:12–13

12: And Jesus entered the temple and drove out all those who sold and bought in the temple, and he overturned the tables of the money-changers and the seats of those who sold pigeons.
13: He said to them, "It is written, 'My house shall be called a house of prayer,' but you make it a den of robbers."

God is the same, and never changes. The God that is in the Old Testament is the same as the God in the New Testament. Jesus did not come here to just talk about love, and how everybody makes it to heaven. Jesus came here to do the will of his Father. Preach the gospel, show us how we should be living and be crucified, unjustly and without sin, so we might have an opportunity to be saved. If you think that you said a magic prayer and now you're going to heaven, you are sorely mistaken. The only way for you to know everything about Jesus, you're going to at least read the New Testament; but, there is also a lot about Jesus in the Old Testament. If you go to church once a week and say a prayer every night, I ask you to get a notebook and a pen and write down everything that you know about Jesus. Then, ask yourself if Jesus appeared to you at that moment would he know you. What I mean by him "knowing you" is what's your relationship with Jesus. Do you talk to him all of the time or just when you need something? Did you learn about him by reading the Bible? Trust me, it is much better for me asking you this than God asking you after you have already died. You still have time. Please, try to know Jesus. If you know him, he is everything you need. God makes you feel a way that nobody can explain.

I just want to add sometimes you just know you are saved. If you feel the Holy Spirit, you love and know Jesus, and you repent for your sins then you should start looking for your calling. My situation was a little different. Jesus did not tell me I was saved, but as soon as I turned into a spirit, I knew by my feelings. I felt the Father, Jesus Christ, and the Holy Spirit. I think about that a lot. When I got home, before I could remember anything about the time I was with Jesus Christ, I knew I was saved. I felt God so powerfully and knew what was right and wrong. All I wanted to do was love and praise God, and I still do.

CHAPTER 8

THE FIGHT NEVER STOPS

I am in no way trying to add to the Bible or God's Word. Over the past five years I have read a lot, watched a lot, felt all different ways, had revelations, dreams, and visions, and I just have a few thoughts. These things were not told to me, all these are things I have seen in my head. They are mostly from the Bible and the information given to me by Jesus Christ. I think it is a possibility that these things may happen.

God knows everyone's heart. God knows that with certain people, no matter how hard he tries to open their eyes, they always choose not to open their eyes. The reason is that they love the world more than anything else. I do believe that as the Second Coming gets closer, you will see a rise in born-again Christians. The reason behind that is God will open all the eyes of people that have a pure, loving heart and are seeking the truth.

John 20:24–29

24: Now Thomas, one of the twelve, called the Twin, was not with them when Jesus came.
25: So the other disciples told him, "We have seen the Lord." But he said to them, "Unless I see in his hands the mark of the nails, and

place my finger into the mark of the nails, and place my hand into his side, I will never believe."

26: Eight days later, his disciples were inside again, and Thomas was with them. Although the doors were locked, Jesus came and stood among them and said, "Peace be with you."

27: Then he said to Thomas, "Put your finger here, and see my hands; and put out your hand, and place it in my side. Do you not disbelieve, but believe."

28: Thomas answered him, "My Lord and my God!"

29: Jesus said to him, "Have you believed because you have seen me? Blessed are those who have not seen and yet have believed."

This tells you how some of us think. Thomas was with Jesus, taught by Jesus, and saw all the miracles that Jesus did. He still did not believe that Jesus was back from the dead and talking to people, even though the apostles were telling him that Jesus was back. Only God truly knows who would believe and who would not. That is our free will. I will guarantee that when Jesus returns, everyone will know immediately. That is why every knee shall bow and every tongue will confess that Jesus Christ is God. I still remember what it felt like. It was embedded in my mind. Just as we blink our eyes and not think about it. So, the truth of God will be in your mind. I do not exactly know how it will happen. For me it was as soon as I went to my spirit. It is very possible that everyone will become their spirit as soon as Jesus returns. That would make the most sense.

John 14:6

6: Jesus said to him, "I am the way, and the truth, and the life. No one comes to the Father except through me.

All that matters is your relationship with Jesus Christ. I do not think most people really understand what is coming. I hear people talk about tribulations, raptures, the end of the world, and they are completely missing the one and only thing that matters. **The fear of GOD.** I also know that many Christians will not believe what I have said. That is your choice. Jesus told me that he died and came back, and people do not believe that either. Jesus also said, "My sheep hear my voice, and I know them, and they follow me" (John 10:27). Some people will never believe. Salvation is between God and you. All I can do is point you toward Jesus. People also tell me we can agree to disagree. My reply is to show me the verse that supports your belief. Then I get no reply. One day at work there were two older people talking about the Catholic religion. They were both Catholic. One was questioning certain things. One thing was the Eucharist taking away sins. He said, "How does this thing take away sins?" I jumped in and I said, "You're right, it doesn't." She turned to me and said, "Oh, I guess you have some phone that you can talk to God with." I simply said that I met Jesus when I died for thirty-five minutes. She just rolled her eyes and I just let them go back and forth. She was rude. Only God can get through to someone like her. Some people would rather go to their death believing something they have no proof of. That just confirmed everything Jesus told me. He will be returning with wrath. Everyone will have their time with the Father during their final judgment. It was upsetting to me. I am just trying to give someone important information, but she just rolled her eyes. Hopefully God will get through to her before it is too late.

Matthew 10:28

28: And do not fear those who kill the body but cannot kill the soul. Rather fear him who can destroy both soul and body in hell.

I knew someone that would never have a lot of money on him. So, I asked him, "Don't you worry if something happens? It is good to hold on to some of your money." He replied to me, "God gives me everything I need." He did not have a fancy car, multiple houses, or any retirement fund. I asked him if he was concerned about retiring one day. He replied, "God will handle my retirement." Then I got a little personal because I did not understand why he lives the way he does. I said I just have one final question. "You make decent money, you're older, why are you single and still living at home with your mother?" He said, "Five years ago my father passed away. My mother came up to me and asked me to help her. She could not get through it alone. She said, 'I will lose the house and need to go to a nursing or assisted-living home. Nobody else will help me." She was crying while she said it. I immediately said, 'Do not worry, I will help you and not leave you alone. I am rich in the most important thing, my faith. My day will come."

Now I look back and say, "That is why God chose me," and I did not even know it. That was literally my first thought. It is what is in your heart. I put my social life or having my own place aside because God tells us to respect our mother and father. On the morning I collapsed and died, who was there to call 911? My mother. Everything happens for a reason. I do not care how this world looks at me. This is not my world. I do not belong here. I do not have much money or a fancy car. God allows me to work with my heart problems, iron-deficiency anemia, chest pain, and it is a fight every day. God provides me with clothes, food, and a place to live. I will be home when I am with God in heaven. If I had money a lot of it would go to the less fortunate. There are two things I will accomplish once this book is a bestseller. That is between Jesus and myself. I am in no way saying I would not get a nice house or a nice car. There are two things I really want to do. I believe they are in my heart for a reason. There are many people that need help and need to hear the gospel of Jesus Christ. Along the way, if God gives me the call to write another book, I will gladly do it. I do not live for anyone on this earth. I also do not care what anyone thinks of me. I do not belong here. I answer to God and God only. I have been married twice, divorced twice. Things just never work out with women for me. I wondered why for a long time. Then, the Word of God tells us how it is supposed to work. God created man. He did not want man to be alone, so God created a woman and used one of man's ribs. She is to be the helper of man. There are very few women that know that or live like that.

1 Corinthians 11:8–9

8: For man was not made from woman, but woman from man.
9: Neither was man created for woman, but woman for man.

I have put many different topics in this book. I explained them the best I could. Just know there are things I mention over and over for a reason. What is truly in your heart? Do you truly know Jesus Christ? If I keep mentioning the same thing, there is a reason why. Think about it. All I ask is if you disagree, that is fine. I am sure many will. Just do not argue about it. That is simply wasting time.

The crazy thing was that this book was written, then I got a vision. It backed up everything I have said. It added some new things also. I remember how Jesus felt like a brother that I have had forever. I also know I am his servant. I really think the five years now has really brought us together on a higher level. Through these years with all the revelations, dreams, visions, and everything else, I was never told anything about the second coming of Jesus Christ. But now, I have seen and heard the truth. Everything is in place and has been prepared. It will happen when the Father is ready. This must put some urgency on your relationships with Jesus Christ. Please, if you know anyone that does not know Jesus, tell them about him or let them read your copy of this book.

The fear of God is gone from this world. I do not see God in my everyday life, on TV, on the Internet; I just do not see where people live their life with the fear of God in them. Since the last dream I got, recently, all I can think about is wanting to be with God. I literally feel like I am stuck between two worlds. My mind is in heaven and my body is on earth. I cannot help but think that something is going to happen soon. Either with me or with this world. From here on, I feel that most people being born now are not going to be told about God at all.

I am very proud of this book. It shows the correct interpretations of the Bible. The Bible does not mention a rapture. I have also shown you what the worst tribulation really was and when it happened. . There is no such thing as a pre or post tribulation rapture. All Satan is doing is taking your time away from doing what you should be doing. Which is to know Jesus Christ and fight for every soul. How much time do people waste on that stuff? Hours and hours. How many souls can you be planting a seed in? I see all these videos about this. Who cares? Jesus Christ is coming, tell someone about how wonderful Jesus is instead. A lot of things had to happen for any of us to be able to go to heaven. God planned a way for us. He gave us a path. Then God had to purchase us at a very high cost. The sacrifice of our Lord and Savior Jesus Christ. Just think, the creator of all things made the way and that is why it is not easy to get to heaven. The Father, who has been with Jesus from the beginning of time, along with the Holy Spirit, had to send his only Son into our world. Jesus wanted to do the will of his Father, so he lowered himself and was born into this world. Jesus had to go through a lot for the glory of his Father. The Father crushed the Son of Man and took all our sins for us. My mind cannot comprehend that here on earth. Once that happened, there was his resurrection. Then Jesus had defeated everything. That is why, when

Jesus Christ returns, he is going to return with power and glory. It is going to be something nobody has ever seen, and everyone is going to see it.

The Second War in Heaven

There are some important things Jesus revealed to me. They were very important to Jesus. The Crucifixion was his ultimate hour. He was doing the will of the Father. After it was completed, Jesus was glorified in many ways. Once he was resurrected, he had just saved billions of people. There was a second war in heaven. I am being honest, I did not know about this. I remember going over this verse, but it slipped my mind. Jesus had taken away the only things left that Satan had power over. The war was about Jesus taking the keys of hell and death away from Satan. Satan also lost his ability to go into heaven and talk to God about people on earth, such as in the book of Job. Michael, the archangel, threw him, and his one-third of angels that followed Satan, out of heaven for the last time. It was a very victorious time for our Lord and Savior. Instead of Satan complaining about people on earth, now we have our ultimate priest and mediator for positive things. Jesus can talk to the Father about positive things about us. I feel so honored to have a King and a Savior that loves me. There is nothing I can ever do to show how much I love him and express my feelings for God the Father, the Savior of everyone, Lord Jesus Christ, and the Holy Spirit that is always guiding me and showing me the correct way to stay on this narrow path.

Revelation 12:7–12

7: Now war arose in heaven, Michael and his angels fighting against the dragon. And the dragon and his angels fought back,

8: but he was defeated, and there was no longer any place for them in heaven.

9: And the great dragon was thrown down, that ancient serpent, who is called the devil and Satan, the deceiver of the whole world—he was thrown down to the earth, and his angels were thrown down with him.

10: And I heard a loud voice in heaven, saying, "Now the salvation and the power and the kingdom of our God and the authority of his Christ have come, for the accuser of our brothers has been thrown down, who accuses them day and night before our God.

11: And they have conquered him by the blood of the Lamb and by the word of their testimony, for they loved not their lives even unto death.

12: Therefore, rejoice, O heavens and you who dwell in them! But woe to you, O earth and sea, for the devil has come down to you in great wrath, because he knows his time is short!"

Jesus destroyed all our enemies for us. Now Jesus has the keys of death and hell. Nothing evil can harm those of us in Christ. Jesus is our mediator to the Father. Satan can no longer walk into heaven and tell God that one of us is doing something wrong. Satan's time is running out. He is going after everyone's weakness. So, always be aware of traps. He has no ability to harm us, but he can still use his angels to influence us. If you're Christian, he will try his hardest to get you off your narrow path. Please be aware of that. Do not be confused about that. It is true, once we are saved by Jesus Christ, Satan cannot do anything to us. But he still can influence us. If you have a best friend, and Satan starts to control him, then he will use that opportunity to influence you. He is not doing anything to us physically, but the spirit world is all around us. More than you could ever imagine. Just watch out for things around you that may influence you.

The book of Revelation is difficult to understand. In my first book, *I Died to Meet Jesus*, I did not have the complete understanding of the book of Revelation interpreted. I obviously did not have it in there about these important topics, but God wanted it in here. I did not understand chapter 12. That one was all Jesus. I will just say it has nothing to do with the message of this book. I would have to explain all of Revelation.

As it turns out, it was very important. I will tell you I remember that day, I will never forget it. Jesus revealed a lot to me that day. A lot of my questions were answered that day and it allowed me to finish this book. It was a regular day. I was praying to Jesus. I was telling him I needed more information about that day I died. I have done that many times. He explained a lot about the day. So, you never know when your prayers will be answered. This was months before my vision of when my body died.

Please try to understand that God loves all of us. There are some verses that you can feel the anger God has toward sin. God is love, he does not want to lose any of us. Please try to take a few minutes. Many years ago, there was God the Father, the Son, and the Holy Spirit. God, the Father, created everything around us through Jesus Christ. God knew us before we were even born. Sin entered his creation and God is love, so he hates sin. Before any of that happened, the Father and the Son created a way so that everyone could be with them. If you have a child or someone very close in your life, think that one day they will have to be sacrificed. Jesus gave up all his power and glory to suffer and die. It was the Father's will to crush him to give all of us an opportunity. Jesus did the will of his Father. That glorified Jesus and now Jesus Christ wants you to know that he provided the only way for all of us.

One morning I woke up, I went into the bathroom to get ready for the day, The next thing I knew was my body was dead. From there I felt the best feeling that I will ever need, God's love. None of us know exactly why, but sometimes God does something just to let you know he is everything. It literally took almost five years to finally have a grasp on everything that happened. It is crazy to think thirty minutes can change everything in your life. Now I feel fulfilled. Everything that happened to me is finally in a book, and it is completed. I know that God has a bunch of things planned for me, but this was the main thing that had to happen. There are a lot of things that I can write about in much more detail, but I'm not thinking about another book for a little while. This is what Jesus wanted me to tell everyone. I really needed all the knowledge and gifts that God gave me. I've tried to explain things by using Bible verses. God's words are what is important, mine mean nothing. The topics I covered are important. The messages I am giving you about the truth or about a rapture, the end of days, and the second coming of Jesus Christ do not matter right now. What is important is your relationship with Jesus Christ. You have to ask yourself, "If I die today, does Jesus know me?" If you are close to Jesus and the Holy Spirit is guiding you, just be ready to help others. When Jesus asked the disciples if they wanted to leave too, Peter said, "Master, to whom would we go? You have the words of real life, eternal life. We've already committed ourselves, confident that you are the holy one of God." You always have to be confident. You must tell people how important Jesus is with authority. I get asked a lot about Jesus because of my tattoos. Sometimes it leads to a ten-minute conversation, others I do not say much, mostly because I am helping multiple people at once. Honestly, sometimes I just do not feel like it. I should never do that, but I sin, and I am just a regular person. I have been trying not to do that because I always feel bad about it later. My relationship with the Holy Spirit, Jesus Christ, and the Father is very strong most of the time. There are days that I do not feel close to God, and I will tell him, pray about it, and read the Bible or write. The best thing you can tell someone is to get to know Jesus. He will change your whole life but be confident. Whatever happens to me means nothing. But what happened to me is a good way that I can get to my main point. We all have our own testimonies. If God helped you through the death of a loved one or helped you through anything difficult, that is your testimony. Most people have a testimony because when you are born again something happens to you.

God's Word is very powerful. There is a lot of proof of that. .. The Old Testament varies but in my opinion the final version was written by God. Between 1200-125BC the Old Testament was being written. The New Testament was written anywhere from AD 30 to AD 70. So, the events of Jesus Christ were written close to his death and resurrection. I know the history books put the ascension of Jesus Christ between AD 30 and AD 36. I always keep a journal. If I saw someone healing everyone and casting demons out, I would be writing it down. You can use AD 70 if you want, close enough to the time of Jesus Christ for me. There are many revelations and prophecies in the Bible, including the prophecy that Jesus Christ would be born hundreds of years before he was. Every prophecy by Jesus Christ happened just as he said it would. The prophecy of the second coming of Jesus Christ does not have a date given. Jesus prophesied that he was going to return after his death, he told everyone about the temple being destroyed, and he also said he is the Way, the Truth, and Life. The only way to the Father and to heaven is through him. The Bible has run through the test of time. Just as Jesus told us. The answer to everything is in the Bible. Please just put an hour a day aside to read it. If you do not understand something, just write down the verse and keep going. The next time you are at church, or Bible study, ask one of the leaders. Talk to God throughout the day. If something nice happens, say "Thank you, God." I find myself thanking God a lot. If someone does something nice for you throughout the day, thank them, then after thank God, because he made it happen. It may sound like a lot, but it isn't. Over time it is second nature, you start doing it automatically.

I've explained all the verses. I gave you an insight as to how God feels. If nothing else, I proved there is a God. Science cannot explain what happened to me. People die every day. Most do not come back. I'm one of the few that knows what happens after you die. Dying for over thirty minutes is not a dream or a vision. It was something that God has been telling me for years about what's going to happen to me. God had it in my thoughts for years that one day I was going to die and come back. I would think about it and wonder what it would be like. It is amazing what God puts in our hearts and thoughts. Sometimes I thought about it, other times it was just a thought that came and went away. I have always had this feeling inside that God was going to use me for something special. Something that does not happen every day. As I got older, I said to myself that it's too late now. I thank God that I was wrong. I always had a close relationship with God the Father. I was not close with Jesus or the Holy Spirit. It was a huge change when I got home from the hospital. I really felt the Father, the Son, and the Holy Spirit. It was very spiritual, and I could still feel being a spirit. It feels so different. We are supposed to pray to God in the spirit, but after being a spirit, it is hard for me to get that feeling back.

The creator of everything told me to do something. This is all God's Word. The Holy Spirit is inside me and I am just a vessel for God to use. I feel honored that God involved me with this. Honestly, I did not feel like that for the first few years after. At least not until fhey found the main cause of the cardiac arrest. I did not want to come back, and I had no idea why God brought me back. Even after I put everything together, I did not know what I was supposed to do with it. I did not think that anyone would believe me, I did not know how I was going to tell anyone, and I wondered why me. This event has changed my life in so many ways. I realized that it has nothing to do with me if someone believes me or not. God handles all that. God reveals what he wants, when he wants. When Jesus lived on this earth, the majority of people could not recognize him as God. If they did, they would not have crucified him. Most people were blinded.

Pray to God for understanding and guidance. I recommend also reading the four Gospels first: Matthew, Mark, Luke, and John. The only reason why I say that is because you can read the words of Jesus Christ. What I did after the Gospels is I wrote the title of each book of the Bible on a piece of paper, put them all in a hat, and picked one at a time to read. I figured that way God was in control of what I read. Read about God and learn from others. Just be careful, there are a lot of wolves in sheep's clothing. Their main purpose is making money. If you go to a place that tells you a watered-down version of the Bible, walk away and never go back. If you look into a church and their main focus is telling you saying a prayer is all you need to do, then stay away. You will be able to tell. I was going to a Catholic church and for years I'd get a lump in my throat as soon as I walked in. I knew something was wrong, I just did not know what. Just find a place that teaches you the Word of God and focuses on Jesus. It does take time and it will not be easy. It is more than worth it. You will always have God with you. He never leaves you.

Matthew 22:37–40

37: And he said to him, "You shall love the Lord your God with all your heart and all your soul and with all your mind.
38: This is the great and first commandment.
39: And a second is like it: You shall love your neighbor as yourself.
40: On these two commandments depend all the Law and the Prophets."

Matthew 5:16

16: In the same way, let your light shine before others, so that they may see your good works and give glory to your Father who is in heaven.

Every good work you do for someone glorifies God. We do not believe in a works-based religion, but it is always good to do things that glorify God. He is deserving of glory and praise. Once you feel his love, that's all you want to do, praise and glorify God. God has created a lot of things, and everything is good. I do not know how God feels about other creations, but he truly loves us. God is love and he never changes, he is also a judge of sin. No matter the sin, God hates it. It really upsets God when people try to make money from him and his word for the wrong reasons. This does not mean that people cannot make a living spreading God's Word. It's the people that do not even care about God and make money from him. False preachers, of which there are plenty of them. The people that misinterpret the Bible and make money from it. They know who they are. Anyone who does not recognize Jesus Christ as God upsets God. The people who are always trying to lead people away from God angers him. God gave us our own will, but we should not be trying to get others to look away from God. So, with knowing all that, it is always good to glorify God whenever we can.

Joel 2:12-13

12: "Yet even now," declares the LORD, "return to me with all your heart, with fasting, with weeping, and with mourning;
13: and rend your hearts and not your garments." Return to the LORD your God, for he is gracious and merciful, slow to anger, and abounding steadfast love; and he relents over disaster.

We also must not give up. If God has your mind on something you must be patient and do not give up. Some nights felt like torture for me. I had no idea why God brought me back and was still facing the same problem with no answers; I was getting worse. My love, faith, and trust in God got me through it. I was starting to get nervous three years ago. The episodes were happening multiple times a day. Then I was suffering from the shocks and the episodes. Once it started happening during physical activity, I really did not think my body could take much more. I started thinking how many times will I get shocked and still be fine. I was thinking one of these times that it just wasn't going to restart my heart. In the hospital I was all for the surgery, the cardiac ablation, but I was looking at it and it's a last resort and would not likely cure the problem. I reached a point that I was not strong enough to handle anymore. I just prayed and told God exactly how I felt. I was raising the white flag and giving up. God picked me up, brushed off the dust. He knew all my faith was in him. He always comes through, always. As soon as they switched my meds, my life changed. It took almost two-and-a-half years. I even reached the point that I was OK if God took me home. So, it takes time sometimes. Shortly after that I knew what I had to do. In my head I could not write the book until all of that was over.

God will help you through the sad, lonely nights. There were times that I would be really depressed, and I'd cry every night for weeks. My journey is still not over. It is just going into a different phase. God pulled off a miracle on me, a few of them, so now I have to inspire others. I have to teach and help others. God got me through everything and made me into a stronger person. I am hoping and praying that God does the same for you. It took five years to be one with God. It was by far the most difficult time I ever went through. People do not know everything about me. There are things I did not want to put into this book for everyone to read. I will do anything for God. Including keeping certain things between us.

Satan was thrown down to earth with one-third of God's angels that followed Satan. He is on a mission to destroy as many souls as possible. This goes back to Satan, being the most powerful angel, thinking he was stronger than God. If he truly thought that it just shows his arrogance and stupidity in my opinion. Regardless, he is powerful and has a lot of angels at his disposal. As Christians, he has no power against us. Jesus destroyed all of our enemies. What he does have is influence. There are different ways he can try to influence you to sin. He is going to try and attack your weakest point. He will use the Internet, TV, all the apps you have access to, and whatever else he can, including other people. You must be aware that bad things are still going to happen to us. We cannot see this war, it is spiritual, but it is there. I can see a lot of it, but it is difficult to see if you were never a spirit. Just because you may be protected, that does not mean everyone around you is. I really do not want to get into everything that Satan is doing, I will just say trust in Jesus Christ, no matter what happens around you or your family. I am not the one who God wants to explain what is around us. Just realize you will be attacked by things that happen around you. The only one you can truly trust is Jesus Christ. He is the way to the Father, so you must trust him.

Revelation 2:10

10: Do not fear what you are about to suffer. Behold, the devil is about to throw some of you into prison, that you may be tested, and for ten days you will have tribulation. Be faithful unto death, and I will give you the crown of life.

You will get attacked all of the time. One bad thing will happen, then another thing, and another. So how do we get through it? Pray to God. When you lay down at night and the mortgage is late, you don't have a lot of food, and your car just broke down, remember

Jesus already defeated the world. Put all your worry and faith in God. The next day you can get a forbearance on that month's mortgage payment, a family member drops off some food, and your neighbor knows someone that can fix the car and you can pay them later. These things do happen when you put everything in God's hands. Lay on that pillow, pray to God, and tell him I know you have all this taken care of. Ask God to take away any fear or doubt you have, and God will respond. I had to go without a car for a month. I had to have the front axle fixed on it and, magically, when he was repairing the front axle that goes into the transmission, the axle got fixed but the transmission went. The mechanic did not take any responsibility for the transmission. He didn't work on transmissions, so he sent it to one of his "buddies'" transmission places and had it for five weeks. I put it in God's hands. Did I get aggravated? A few times, yes! I just trusted God and kept praying. It took a lot of walking and a lot of Ubers, but I got the car back. I was also in the hospital for one of those weeks, so it was not an easy time. The more I trust God, the more he does for me. So, now, If I really need something, for something positive, God always comes through.

1 Thessalonians 5:17–18

17: pray without ceasing,
18: give thanks in all circumstances; for this is the will of God in Christ Jesus for you.

So, I died and was in the presence of Jesus, but I still have as many problems as everyone else. My father passed away six months before I died. Then, after that, I died and came back. It was a very difficult time for me. I have mostly kept to myself. I went through the majority of this with God. Some nights I felt alone, but that brought me closer to God. Now, I am stronger than ever. Not because of anything

I did, but because I trust God 100 percent with everything. I love him, trust him, live for him, and I rose with him and will again. God molds us with many different things. If there is nothing bad ever happening to you, I would be very concerned. Satan is not going to attack someone he already has. I live to serve God. My testimony of what God did for me is the best weapon I have. In the right situation it can help. I pray that God will use it. This may sound stupid, but I always viewed one day being a soldier for Jesus. This is a war for souls. We must bring God's kingdom here. "On earth as it is in heaven." I am not far off from my dream. The only difference is that this war is fought with words, not swords. That makes sense to me now. There is nothing more powerful than the Word of God. "In the beginning was the Word, and the Word was with God, and the Word was God."

Satan Tried to Prevent This Book

I am not spending a long time on this, but I feel like I must mention it. There were times that I almost died in the past.

In 2006, I had abdominal surgery because I was getting chronic pain in my abdomen. Scar tissue was removed. Six months later, they took my gallbladder out. Immediately following the surgery, I told them something did not feel right. They said it was just from the air they use to do the surgery. I just had abdominal surgery six months before that, and it did not feel like that. I had severe pain in my abdomen. They released me. That night I was in severe pain and did not sleep. In the morning I called the surgeon to tell him it did not feel right. He told me it was probably from normal surgery and gave me a stronger painkiller. I made it through that night, but the severe pain was getting worse. As that day went on all I could do was just keep walking around the house. It literally felt like someone stabbed me in the back and was turning the knife over and over. I started sweating and noticed my breathing was getting worse. This was now the third

day, and I literally could not take the pain anymore. I went by res-
cue to the nearest hospital. They gave me stronger pain medication
and did a CT scan. I told them nothing was helping, and it hurt with
every breath I took. They said it looked like my whole abdomen was
filled with air. They rushed me to the original hospital. They gave me
morphine and something else. Finally, I did get some relief from the
pain and slept for two hours. I told them the pain was coming back
again. Finally, at around 9:00 p.m. the surgeon came in and said I
had to have surgery again. They did emergency surgery that night.
I remember waking up not knowing what day it was and thinking I
was going to have the surgery. It was already completed. What happened is when they closed off the cystic duct to my gallbladder, it did
not completely close. The surgeon said I had bile in my whole abdomen and around my lungs. He also said he was surprised that I was
still alive.

I had to have a drainage tube in me for four weeks. The tube hurt.
That was one of several times I almost died. I was on strong pain
meds for almost eight months at that time. They had to do the surgery again about six months later because of the scar tissue. Not too
long after that I had a hernia and partial blockage of my intestines. In
the end, I had four abdominal surgeries over two years, and I was on
pain medication the whole time. When you have been on them that
long, it is very difficult to get off them.

I ended up having chronic abdominal pain and saw a pain man-
agement specialist. Let's just say I was put on every narcotic pain re-
liever at some point. That led to multiple problems. I did not know
how I got through that alive, but now I know how I got through it.
Over the next few years there were a couple of times I should have
died. God told Satan, "You cannot have this one." That was a dark time
in my life. I kept close to God, but I was still Catholic, was not born
again, and did not know Jesus Christ.

Looking back, God was preparing me for everything that was going to happen. This is just the beginning of my journey with God. I took Satan's hardest hit and kept going. I can relate to many people. I know what is like to be alone, depressed, fighting battle after battle. God decided it was my time to do work for his kingdom. The Holy Spirit can give you so much strength. All these things happened for a reason. God's hand is all over my life. This is why I have always felt different. I cannot relate to this world. I feel like I am different from a lot of people. I have always felt it and I had a huge void in my life. I felt home and normal when I was with Jesus Christ. It was beyond worth it.

Everyone has problems in their life. Some people have severe physical issues, some are struggling to keep a roof over their heads, and I can go on and on. The one thing that is different is you. We are all different. Just think of this for a minute, God created every one of us with different fingerprints and DNA. I do not know how science could explain that one. Each of us has our own issues, but we were also created by a loving God. A God that is perfect in every way, has three Persons that affect us in different ways, and created you for a reason. The glory of God. He is counting on you to get involved and do what you were created for. The only way you can know what that is is by knowing him. Above all, you must know God. The Father draws us in, Jesus Christ saves us, then the Holy Spirit guides us. That is exactly what happened to me. We all have our own way. Then, once you know Jesus, he will refine you and make you the strongest you can be. You will have the power of God inside you. That means you can do whatever God puts in your heart to do. As a child of God, after we are saved, we will still fall down. If you have 100 percent faith in God, he will get you up every time. Then you can reach a level where you are connected with God, and he will carry you on the right path. All I want is to be in his presence. I want to be with God. I still have things God wants me to do. He knows I love him above all. I can understand why Abraham did what God told him to do. My love is that strong for God. I know people will say it is because I died and was in the presence of Jesus Christ. But I truly believe that anyone can get to that point.

Genesis 22:2

2: He said, "Take your son, your only son Isaac, whom you love, and go to the land of Moriah, and offer him there as a burnt offering on one of the mountains of which I shall tell you."

Abraham showed that he had 100 percent faith in God. He brought his son there and was about to kill his son, then an angel of God stepped in and stopped it. Many years later, God the Father was faced with the same exact thing, Jesus Christ sacrificed himself for all of us. Everything happens for a reason. That reason is the glory of God.

Everyone has the choice to take the easy path that leads to eternity in hell or the difficult path that leads to an eternity with God. There is no other way I can tell you. It is worth any sacrifice to take the narrow, difficult, but rewarding path. Being in the presence of God feels . . . it is worth dying for, twice or as many times it takes.

When I got the vision, it was as if it was happening when I saw it. God loves us, more than you can ever imagine. He had been thinking about it for at least five years. God's judgment is close. Jesus felt as if he had dealt with it already. He did not seem upset at all when he was talking to me. Now we know the Father is ready for our final judgment. It is bright again in heaven. The Father is excited to be with all his children. Jesus is excited because he will show the world his glory, power, and everyone will know he is God. I have told you everything God wanted me to tell you. Now, it is your choice; salvation is between you and God.

I pray that God blesses you with knowing him. After you are saved, trust God with everything, know him, talk to him, praise him, and you will feel his presence. The ultimate key is Jesus Christ. Always look toward him. It does not matter how bad it gets.

Feeling the love and protection of God is worth going through anything. This life is a drop in the bucket compared to eternity. God has more things for us to do after our bodies die here. There is a plan for each of us.

1 John 4:4

4: Little children, you are from God and have overcome them, for he who is in you is greater than he who is in the world.

CHAPTER 9

THE FINAL CHAPTER—THE RETURN OF JESUS CHRIST:

The Wrath Is Coming

If I take out everything Jesus told me, it does not change anything. Jesus will return at some point. You can believe what you want about the Rapture, the end of the age, and that still does not change the fact that Jesus will return. Everyone will be judged. Salvation is between you and God. What this book is telling you is to believe in the correct Jesus Christ. If you believe that Jesus cannot take away all your sins and you need purgatory, that is the wrong Jesus. If you believe that Jesus is not God, is Satan's brother, or was just a mighty prophet, you do not believe in the correct Jesus. If you think Jesus will forgive everyone, that is definitely the wrong Jesus. We may not have a lot of time. I can see all the activity going on all around us. It is truly amazing how God knows everything about every person, angel, and even animal. We all have our own book. God is very organized. Our book has everything we have ever done and thought. That is the guarantee that God knows everything about us, and what is in our heart, for Judgment Day. There is an angel, right now, that is writing down everything about you. This is how precise God is. Everything, good or evil, is being written down. Everyone has their own book. During our final judgment, your book will be in God's hands. Good and bad, but if you are saved by Jesus Christ, all the bad is washed away. He knows our sins no more. They are all gone. That is just a small bit of knowledge about the spirit world. Just think of that. What is in your book? Has it been wiped clean by the blood of Jesus Christ? Just think about it for a while. This truly is a war. It is happening all around us. It affects all of us. A soul is precious. It is eternal. So you will be you, forever. Would you rather live eternity with all the positive things in your life, or all the negative?

Matthew 24:30–31

30: Then will appear in heaven the sign of the Son of Man, and then all the tribes of the earth will mourn, and they will see the Son of Man coming on the clouds of heaven with power and great glory.
31: And he will send out his angels with a loud trumpet call, and they will gather his elect from the four winds, from one end of heaven to the other.

Words from Jesus Christ to me: "Now the table is set. Once all the guests arrive, then I will arrive."

As I kept looking back at what Jesus Christ told me, all the knowledge that he gave me, all the revelations and visions and dreams, this was the ultimate message from Jesus Christ. He is coming back, and everyone will be judged. The messages have been sent out. All the prophets have spoken, Jesus Christ has spoken, and the return of Jesus Christ will be soon because of the many things I mention in this book. The biggest thing that tells us that the time is near is that God has been taken out of everything and the world does not fear the wrath of God anymore. On top of that, most people believe that God is just going to take everyone to heaven. The two biggest holidays are Christmas and Easter and, at one point, those days really meant something. The birth of Jesus Christ into his own creation, and then the resurrection of Jesus Christ three days after the Crucifixion, meant something to people. How many kids know why we celebrate those two days? Our society has relied on forty-five minutes a week to teach their kids about God, and the parents have no clue about God. After a Catholic Mass, ask the people if they read the Bible. They may say yes because they do not want to feel awkward about that question after church, but most do not read it on a regular basis.

Therefore, God Gave Them up to Their Desires

2 Timothy 3:1–7

1: But understand this, that in the last days there will come times of difficulty.
2: For people will be lovers of self, lovers of money, proud, arrogant, abusive, disobedient to their parents, ungrateful, unholy,
3: heartless, unappeasable, slanderous, without self-control, brutal, not loving good,
4: treacherous, reckless, swollen with conceit, lovers of pleasure rather than lovers of God,
5: having the appearance of godliness, but denying its power. Avoid such people.
6: For among them are those who creep into households and capture weak women, burdened with sins and led astray by various passions,
7: always learning and never able to arrive at a knowledge of the truth.

It is very sad to read those verses. The problem is that is exactly the way life is right now. In verse 2, this is exactly what is going on with the Internet right now. Facebook, TikTok, and YouTube are just a very small part of what proves this verse to be happening right now. All people care about is "views" and how they can make themselves popular, because they love themselves that much. The world today loves money; it seems like many kids do not obey their parents. And with most people, there is no making them happy; they are ungrateful of all of these things that God provides us with every day. People have air to breathe, there is plenty of food to eat, a large percentage of people have clothes and a roof over their heads. The problem is they always want more. They want a bigger house, an expensive car, more luxuries and, I do not know how to put it, but everyone just wants more stuff. I saw it every day at work. People are constantly just buying more and more things that do not matter; they are trying to make themselves happy with better things. The truth is that people are unholy and do not have God in their lives; if they did, none of this stuff would matter to them.

God normally puts good desires in our hearts. He will give us desires that will extend God's kingdom and glory. The one thing that all of us must worry about is when God gives in to us and allows us to do what our hearts desire. It's not as if God is putting evil desires in our hearts, he just stops putting desires into our hearts. That is exactly what is happening today. People will look around and ask where God is with all this violence and evilness happening all around us? Those are the people that have to look at themselves in the mirror and answer the main question, "Does Jesus Christ know me?" One way you could answer that question is to think to yourself, "If Jesus appeared to me right now, would this be the first time I'd be talking to him?" Right now, Jesus is my best friend. I talk to him every day. I would be lost without him. To me, Jesus is my king, he is my brother, and he is my best friend. Now nobody can take that away from me. The Father's hands are around me also. There is nothing or nobody that can change it. Once you are saved, you are one of God the Father's children. This is why so many people will be at his feet and he will tell you, "I never knew you; depart from me."When Jesus first came to earth, it was to do the will of his Father in heaven. When he returns, he will return as God, showing his power and glory.

Jeremiah 29:11–13

11: For I know the plans I have for you, declares the LORD, plans for welfare and not for evil, to give you a future and a hope.
12: Then you will call upon me and come and pray to me, and I will hear you.
13: You will seek me and find me, when you seek me with all your heart.

It doesn't seem like God is asking for too much. He is asking us to seek him with all our hearts and pray to him. That is the issue now. Nobody seeks God anymore. Even if they do seek him, they do not do it with all their heart. Our society wants everything right now. We want to say a prayer before we go to sleep and ask for things, and then if we don't get it the next day, we give up. God is talking about seeking him with all your heart and not because you want things. Throughout the Bible there aren't many verses that talk about praying to God for worldly things. God is talking to his children that know him, that love him, and are saved. Those prayers are about helping to grow the kingdom of God. Prayers of forgiveness and more knowledge about God. This is why you cannot read a few verses of the Bible and not consider everything that comes before it and everything that comes after it. There are things that I really want to do, so I pray to God; but what I'm praying for is a way for me to help less-fortunate people, people that are all alone and do not have a family. That is what praying is for. It is for helping us to become more like Jesus; a lot of people pray for understanding the Word of God or they pray for someone that is sick. When you are praying for a new car, God isn't going to move mountains so that you can have a brand-new car. If we're praying for things that we want to enjoy this world, that is going against what the Bible has told us.

This is a difficult chapter for me to write. It is probably because sometimes I can feel how God feels. But it is one of the most important chapters. Jesus Christ is coming back. When I look around the world around me, I do not see God anywhere. I see road rage, violence, people promoting sin and having no fear about their actions. You hear it at so many funerals. They are going to a better place. They are with God now or they are in heaven. I know that is not the time to bring it up, but are you sure that is where they went? You can say that to make yourself feel better, but it is not the truth. That is between God and the person that died. The feeling that I am getting from God is that, based on the population of the world right now, it is actually worse than right before the Flood. What I mean by that is there are more people on the earth right now that are not of God. There are much more saved people right now because it was only Noah before the Flood.

Revelation 12:12

12: Therefore, rejoice, O heavens and you who dwell in them! But woe to you, O earth and sea, for the devil has come down to you in great wrath, because he knows that his time is short!"

After our Lord and Savior, Jesus Christ, defeated all our enemies and took the keys of death and hell from Satan, the second war in heaven took place. Satan and all his angelswere thrown out of heaven for the final time, never to return. Now, we have Jesus as our mediator to God, and Satan knows he does not have much time. He is going to use everything at his disposal to take as many souls as he can with him to hell. If you are not saved by Jesus Christ, you do not have his protection. Just as when Jesus Christ was born into this world, there was a huge rise in demonic possessions; it will happen again as his return gets closer. We are already seeing it. In some of these mass killings, the killer said they blacked out and did not know what was happening or they took their life. It will happen more and more. What Satan is trying to do is kill someone, so they do not have another chance to be saved.

It's Time to Fight Back

A lot of you are going to be looking for any verse to prove that I am wrong. Let me ask you this, "What will that accomplish?" Jesus can come back in 100 years; the purpose of all of this is to get people to want to save souls. All I am doing is showing you what is happening around us. There is still time though. The people that are saved have the power of Jesus Christ to use against evil. We need to use it and fight.

Hebrews 9:28

28: so Christ, having been offered once to bear the sins of many, will appear a second time, not to deal with sin but to save those who are eagerly waiting for him.

2 Peter 3:9

9: The Lord is not slow to fulfill his promise as some count slowness, but is patient toward you, not wishing that any should perish, but that all should reach repentance.

James 5:19–20

19: My brothers, If anyone among you wanders from the truth and someone brings him back,
20: let him know that whoever brings back a sinner from his wandering will save his soul from death and will cover a multitude of sins.

So how do we fight back? With the most powerful thing we have on this earth. The Word of God. The Word of God can break through anything. If someone is drowning in sin, use the powerful words of God and help release him from his sins. Jesus Christ can do anything. He has no boundaries, no enemy that he has not destroyed, and wants to save people.

Matthew 24:42–44

42: Therefore, stay awake, for you do not know on what day your Lord is coming.
43: But know this, that if the master of the house had known in what part of the night the thief was coming, he would have stayed awake and would not have let his house be broken into.
44: Therefore you also must be ready, for the Son of Man is coming at an hour you do not expect.

That will be a beautiful moment. To know that Jesus Christ, who means everything to me, is coming to get me and all of God's children. I think of that every day. My mind cannot comprehend what it will look or feel like, but I know it will be Jesus Christ. This has been a very difficult, challenging, and unbelievable five years for me. God has fulfilled me in every way and has taught me to trust him with everything. From dying for thirty-five minutes, getting shocked eight times, fighting through anemia, surgery, having depression, anxiety, PTSD, and Jesus teaching me to give it all to him is a true blessing. All the knowledge, revelations, visions, dreams, and knowing and seeing what others cannot. They are all blessings from God. I needed all of it to complete this book. So much has happened to me in the last five years and I would not change anything. Jesus has refined and molded me for what is to come. I did not go through all of this just for me. It is all for the glory of God.

Only you can decide what you want. Is it the pleasures of this world? Is it another religion? I would urge you to read the Bible without any prejudice. Pray to God to help you understand the truth. I was not a Christian when I died. I did not know Jesus Christ, but that is who was there when I died. The love he has for each of us cannot be measured or comprehended. It is all you will ever want or need. That is why so many died for believing in him. Once you feel him, you will also not care about dying. You will not be ashamed or try to hide your faith. I know it is difficult, but everything changes when you're born again. You feel God's love. Then you will be complete.

Our Free Will

At the end of the day, we decide what we choose to believe. There is no special Bible verse, there is no special prayer, that can force you to believe in Jesus Christ. Nothing is like that. What happens most of the time is we get caught up with life. We have to work, we have to take care of our families, then it is time to go to sleep. You get so caught up with your life, you do not have time to spend with God. That is exactly what Satan is counting on. Do you watch TV every day? Do you look at your phone? My phone tells me how long I was on my cell phone for the week. It tells me the average time per day and the top three apps. I was even surprised. It is three hours per day. I would have never guessed that. I try to spend at least two hours a day with God. That doesn't include me talking to God all day. Why am I wasting almost three hours a day on the phone? I have to do some self-reflection. I can use more time with God. It is not that bad though. I remembered, an hour of that is listening to music while working out. Which makes me want to ask a question. When I work out, 25 percent of it is gospel songs. The rest is not gospel. I asked myself if it's bad that I listen to the world's music so much. That was my answer. If I must ask if something is bad, then most times it is. I will work on that.

It is like anything else. If you really want to do something, you will find time. It is totally up to you. Everyone does have a choice. One thing I just cannot understand is, "Doesn't everyone think about what happens when we die?" It must cross your mind. When you go to the beach or a park, do you wonder who created all these things? Who created us? If you really want to know the truth, every answer is in the Bible. You can see physical and mental changes when someone is born again. We all cannot deny the changes. No other religion changes a person completely like being born again. This is when you are born of the Holy Spirit. The spirit of God enters you and everything is completely different. Anyone can get this done at a Christian church, but you must want it. You will notice your sins; you will recognize Jesus Christ as God. If you are wondering about it, just try it. Find a Christian church and read a little bit of the Bible. Check out the words in red. Those are words that Jesus Christ spoke while he was here. If you are interested in any of that, the Father is pulling you towards him and his son, Jesus Christ. This is a very good thing. But you must not give in to the desires of this world. You cannot love both. You must choose between the world and Jesus Christ. It is up to you.

This world is a fight. The battle will constantly go on. I have been through a lot in this life. I will list the things that happened over the last five years. Just remember, a lot of people went through a lot worse than I did.

Six months before I died, my father passed away. From that day on, I knew that I had to be there for my mother. This life never gave me anything to truly be happy about, except for my son.

In 2018, I had to deal with PTSD which gave me panic attacks, depression, nightmares, and got worse when the device started shocking me. At the same time, I developed iron-deficiency anemia which was something new and really difficult for me physically. I was tired all the time, was having issues working out; this made my depression worse.

In May of 2020, I was admitted to RI Hospital due to all the episodes I was having. It was a daily event, sometimes multiple times per day. This was causing my heart to stop so the shocks increased. Every day I was worried about 3,000 volts running directly to my heart. It was very painful and scary. I trusted God, but I had to have an honest conversation with him. I was praying and I told God that I could not take it anymore. I sincerely asked God to take me or cure me. I could not live like that anymore. I was suffering. I was very honest. Two days later, the problem was fixed.

In July of 2022, my shoulder gave out. The tendon snapped; I had severe bursitis and osteoarthritis. I was facing surgery and a twelve-month recovery.

Eight months into my recovery I was finally feeling good. I was back at the gym. I was getting bigger and stronger. For three months I had a sinus infection. On March 9, 2023, I went to get antibiotics for my sinuses because that would make me feel better. I was going for a CT scan in a few days. That's when I found out I had COVID.

On January 10, .I still have several health problems to face. I just keep moving forward

Honestly, all the years before that was not much better. If all of this was presented to me years ago, before I died, I would ask myself, "Why would I even bother?" I was always sick with something. I missed my last year of high school with CFS or chronic fatigue syndrome and mononucleosis. I got divorced twice. So I've been alone, sick, and miserable for many years. Would I really say why even bother? Those thirty minutes. I can easily say those thirty minutes are worth all of that and much more. This was prophesied to me years ago. I kept thinking, every night for years, about me dying. Then I meet Jesus Christ and he gives me something important to come back and do. I never knew how it really felt to be with Jesus Christ when I would think about it, nobody can. That is reserved for when you are with Jesus Christ. Now that I know how it feels, I want everyone to feel it. Sometimes I think about when I am with Jesus again, but I also know that it can wait. I still have things to do. When things get difficult, I know there is a reason.

I would not change anything. After I died, I told God I would do anything he wanted me to do. Once I died, I wanted to stay, so it does not matter what happens to me. I know the love of God is waiting for me in heaven. Did I get frustrated or upset when these other things happened? Yes. I am ready to do God's work, not struggle through work and all these things. There is one thing that happens after all these things are done. I feel closer to God, and I feel stronger and stronger. Now I can relate to even more people with each thing I go through. It also allows you to see that the fight still goes on. Once you are born again, you have an **X** on your back. Satan wants to defeat all of God's children. Jesus will not allow that, nor the Father. That will not make him stop trying.

We are not being prepared for just this world. God has plans for all of us. We are not going to heaven and just looking at the scenery all day. Our minds cannot comprehend the knowledge, or the plans, God has for each of us. I just know it is for things that we cannot even think about. That is why these 80–100 years are so important. Eternity is impossible to comprehend. I was thinking that one day, 1,000 years from now, we will look back on this experience. Our minds are much stronger as a spirit. Whenever you get upset, whenever you are wondering why something bad is happening or you feel alone, just remember it is impossible for you to be alone. It is impossible for you to be going through something alone.

Make no mistake about it, everyone will know when Jesus Christ comes to earth again. The first time Jesus came to fulfill all prophecies, he came to do the will of the Father and suffer for all our sins.

Jesus was the only one that is pure and without sin. The second coming of Jesus Christ will be like nothing we have ever seen before. This time he is coming with glory and power like no one has ever seen.

Matthew 24:30–31

30: Then will appear in heaven the sign of the Son of Man, and then all the tribes of the earth will mourn, and they will see the Son of Man coming on the clouds of heaven with power in great glory.
31: And he will send out his angels with a loud trumpet call, and they will gather his elect from the four winds, from end of heaven to the other.

Jesus is coming with authority. This is his moment. Everything that happened from the Old Testament to the New Testament pointed to Jesus Christ. The world did not get to see Jesus in his glory. He destroyed every enemy and now he is presenting the Father with all his children. Jesus had to do a lot. He had to refine us, save us, give us his righteousness, and he did it all for love. These next three verses explain it very well. You must realize everyone is just living their lives. They have no clue. So, our king makes an entrance like no other.

Luke 21:25–26

25: And there will be signs in sun and moon and stars, and on the earth distress of nations in perplexity because of the roaring of the sea and the waves,
26: people fainting with fear and with foreboding of what is coming on the world. For the powers of the heavens will be shaken.
27: And then they will see the Son of Man coming in a cloud with power and great glory.

Well, that tells you that a lot is going to happen all at once. A lot of people will be scared because they do not believe in Jesus Christ. I really feel like those people are going to have so much fear because they will realize the truth. They will be beyond shocked because they thought they would have more time or believed that God was taking everyone to heaven. Unfortunately for many people, they will now know that they will be going to hell. I really do get upset about the billions of people that do not know Jesus Christ, but then I look at the other side of it, everybody has the same chance. Anybody who reads and believes in the Old Testament must know that Jesus Christ is the Savior. That is what the majority of the Old Testament tells people. It tells you who is coming, where he is being born, when he is coming, and even what he's going to do once Jesus gets here.

There are two things that I really want to do. It will be a dream come true because I know God would do this for me. First, I want to see the Father. I want to worship and see the Father, including his face. Second, I want to just sit down with Jesus Christ in a beautiful place and ask him questions. I have so many questions for Jesus. I know I will do that in the future. I know I will be able to do both things because God's love for us is so strong. These are the things I think of. God is everything to me. I pray that everyone will reach this level.

The second coming of Jesus Christ Is well-documented in the Bible. The question that God wants me to address is, "Why is it a big deal?" All of us should be waiting for Jesus to arrive and be doing God's will. You can die in the next minute or Jesus can come back in the next minute. It should not affect our daily responsibilities or our relationship with God. When I really sit and think about God, with everything I went through, and with how close I am with God, I just want to be with him. It will be soon. Those that are saved will understand. Until then, we just must do God's will.

This is one of the last things that have been prophesied in the Bible. Many people view this as a wonderful time. It is going to be a surreal and beautiful time. At the same time, it is going to be a very scary and dreadful time for many people. At that moment, everyone will know that Jesus Christ is our Lord and Savior and our king and all of us are his servants. Also, at that time, many people will realize that they are going to hell for eternity. That is why this is an important event to go over. None of us have any idea when Jesus will be returning, so we still have some time to try to preach the gospel to everyone.

Revelation 1:7

7: Behold, he is coming with the clouds, and every eye will see him, even those who pierced him, and all tribes of the earth will wail on account of him. Even so. Amen

Just think of that for a few minutes. Everyone, even the ones who pierced him, will see him. To me, that is a powerful verse.

Matthew 24:44

44: Therefore you also must be ready, for the Son of Man is coming at an hour you do not expect.

1 Thessalonians 5:2

2: For you yourselves are fully aware that the day of the Lord will come like a thief in the night.

These two verses tell you a lot. There are others that are very similar. The biggest thing that you should learn from these verses is that there will be no warning. There are always going to be wars going on all over the place; you are seeing earthquakes and volcanic eruptions happening everywhere at the same time. These verses are saying that it is just going to be a regular day, just like today, and there will be no warning. Jesus compared it to the days of the Flood. People will just be living their normal lives. That is why I said most of the things that happened in Revelation have already happened. There are always famines, wars, earthquakes, volcanic eruptions going on. This is why we have no idea when the end of the world is going to happen. If there was going to be a rapture, these verses would not make sense. People would still be wondering why millions of people just disappeared or many would convert to Christianity and know Jesus was coming soon. Essentially, the world as we know it will be coming to an end when Jesus Christ comes again. God's Word is very powerful.

John 14:1–3

1: "Let not your hearts be troubled. Believe in God; believe also in me.
2: In my Father's house are many rooms. If it were not so, would I have told you that I go to prepare a place for you?
3: And if I go and prepare a place for you, I will come again and will take you to myself, that where I am you may be also.

Matthew 24:42–44

42: Therefore, stay awake, for you do not know on what day your Lord is coming.
43: But know this, that if the master of the house had known in what part of the night the thief was coming, he would have stayed awake and would not have let his house be broken into.
44: Thereforeyou also must be ready, for the Son of Man is coming at an hour you do not expect.

Satan's Final Opportunity

There will be several things happening that will let you know it is close. It will not be obvious at first. The spirit world will enter the physical world. Satan is going to give it his one last shot. He cannot do it until the time is near. He will release his demons in hell to possess the weak-minded on earth and cause death all around us. You are starting to see it now. These demons will possess people to kill many more. You see it now with the school shootings and all these active-shooter situations. The logic behind this is that a dead person cannot be saved.

The only problem with that is God will not just sit back and let it happen. Once these demons are dealt with here, they cannot come back. They go to hell for eternity. I have mentioned multiple times that there are things going on that we cannot see. Jesus Christ will be sending out his soldiers to try to get to these demons before they can do anything. There are also other ways we will be fighting back, but I cannot go into that. Bottom line, you will see a rise in demonic activity, just as when Jesus Christ was here. While Jesus was spreading his gospel, there was a lot of this going on.

Now, this is a lot of verses all about one incident. I need to put this in to prove my point.

Mark 5:7–13

7: And crying out with a loud voice, he said, "What have you to do with me, Jesus, Son of the Most High God? I adjure you by God, do not torment me."

8: For he was saying to him, "Come out of the man, you unclean spirit!"

9: And Jesus asked him, "What is your name?" He replied, "My name is Legion, for we are many."

10: And he begged him earnestly not to send them out of the country.

11: Now a great herd of pigs was feeding there on the hillside,

12: and they begged him, saying, "Send us to the pigs; let us enter them."

13: So he gave them permission. And the unclean spirits came out and entered the pigs; and the herd, numbering about two thousand, rushed down the steep bank and drowned in the sea.

Here we see 2,000 demons in one person. They knew that he was Jesus Christ, the Son of God, and begged him not to send them far. Jesus could have sent them to hell if he wanted to. Let's look at the planning that Satan has been doing to make this happen and not cause worldwide panic. He desensitized all of us. The first school shooting was a big deal, and the first few mass shootings were a big deal. It entered into our society and then you started seeing it in movies, then television shows. Now it literally happens all the time and we have accepted it as a normal thing that happens. When it hits on a massive scale, the world will not panic. This is just one thing Satan will do. I do not know how he will know when the second coming of Jesus Christ will be. But this has already started. Attendance at church has dropped dramatically since the COVID pandemic and has not recovered. This will continue to get worse. Both of these things will continue. These are some of the last things Satan is doing, but it will get much worse.

There will also be an increase in born-again Christians. Jesus will save all that the Father has written in the Book of Life. Once that is complete, then Jesus Christ will return.

This is a day that Jesus is really looking forward to. The Father is also going to be happy that this day is here. It's going to be different. The children of God will all be very excited, there will be so much to look forward to. I keep telling Jesus that I want a few hours with him because I have so many questions. I will tell you this, a lot of our questions will be answered once this is all complete. I've mentioned before how much knowledge you have when you are in your spirit. All that knowledge we're going to get all at once and a lot of our questions will be answered in our own minds. There is a lot that I'm looking forward to, but this is not the time to focus on that. We must give the people that do not know any of this an opportunity to be able to hear it. God will put us at the right place and at the right time and the Holy Spirit will start to speak, and that's how it's done.

Matthew 24:37–42

37: For as were the days of Noah, so will be the coming of the Son of Man.
38: For as in those days before the flood they were eating and drinking, marrying and giving in marriage, until the day when Noah entered the ark,
39: and they were unaware until the flood came and swept them all away, so will be the coming of the Son of Man.
40: Then two men will be in the field; one will be taken and one left.
41: Two women will be grinding at the mill; one will be taken and one left.
42: Therefore, stay awake, for you do not know on what day your Lord is coming.

That sounds like the second coming of Jesus Christ. It does not in any way sound like some rapture event. We really must read our Bible and be careful what other people say. This also proves that there is no tribulation or anything major happening around the world when he arrives. So, if you were hoping some big event was going to happen and Jesus was going to come and rapture his people off the earth, that is also not credible.

The biggest thing is that the gospel of Jesus Christ has reached the entire world. Now I can look at what was going on before the Flood. Nobody wanted God in their life. They were happy in their sexual immorality and promoting it. Once the United States turned its back on God, I think that started the clock. If you go back even fifty years, we were a God-fearing country. We had prayer in schools; gender identity was not heard of. Things God calls an abomination were not allowed or promoted. We took prayer out of schools, which led to massive school shootings. We made it legal to terminate 50 million unborn souls every year; it is legal for same-sex marriages to get the same benefits as married men and women. There is a lot of violence and now, phones, apps, and TVs take up our whole day. There is no room for God. We shut him out.

God is at the point where he can look down on earth and say, "What is the point? My children are trying, but nobody is listening." I think once the unsaved people reach a certain percentage, compared to saved people, then it is over. These people just do not understand how a fully saved community would live. God will receive constant worship, and everyone would live in peace. I will be looking back on creation, how Moses, Daniel, Noah, and many more lived. I want to see Jesus when he lived on earth. Watching him preach, heal people, and perform miracles. When I think of heaven, that is what I think of. I truly believe God will let us see that. There are two things that I really want to do. It will be a dream come true because I know God would do this for me. First, I want to see the Father. I want to worship and see the Father, including his face. Second, I want to just sit down with Jesus Christ, in a beautiful place, and ask him questions. I have so many questions for Jesus. I know I will do that in the future.

The Wrath Is Coming

Jesus Christ told me how angry the Father is. When he looks at all of us, he sees billions of people ignoring him every day. Once Jesus Christ returns, the Great White Judgment will occur. After all of God's children are in the air with Jesus Christ, everyone left is getting judged. God will bring out your book and will be able to point out every bad thought, every sin, and anything evil that you have done. He will show you when one of his servants tried to talk to you about Jesus Christ. The lake of fire is waiting. If your name is not written in the Book of Life, you cannot enter heaven, ever. God never changes. God never lies. God's Word is permanent. This is "God's wrath" that is coming when Jesus Christ comes back. I pray that everyone believes in Jesus Christ and believes that he came here as a sacrifice for all sinners. God entered his own creation to save us. You must believe that Jesus Christ is God!; He was crucified without cause, died, rose on the third day, and sits at the right hand of God. You also must repent for all your sins. This wrath is coming soon. There is little time. I have done what Jesus Christ asked of me. Now it is between you and Jesus Christ. Please find him.

I will leave everyone with this. If you are born again and know Jesus, it does not even matter what happens next. You cannot control the next five minutes, never mind if a worldwide event happens. Keep trying to point people to Jesus Christ. But do not do it in fear. We cannot tell people that there is no time left, so they have to find Jesus. Our job is to bring the gospel of Jesus Christ to people. We tell people our experiences or things we have seen. I urge all of you to find Jesus Christ. Repent to Jesus Christ, try to be like him. Love God with all your heart, mind, and soul. Love your neighbor as yourself. Love him by learning everything you can about him. Normally, once you accept Jesus Christ as your Lord and Savior, you are blessed with the Holy Spirit. If you did not receive the Holy Spirit, you must find a Christian church that will baptize you with the Holy Spirit.

Today, I found out there is a problem with my lower back. My L3–L4 and L4–L5 disks need to be fixed. God makes all things new. God is in control. Whatever happens is God's will. The pain has been getting worse and worse. I also have a growth in my lung. It is making it difficult for me to go to work. I tell you these things because this life is difficult for everyone, Eternity with God will not come easy. You have to keep looking forward and fight for the Kingdom of God. I keep moving forward telling everyone how wonderful Jesus Christ really is. If I have air in my lungs, I will tell everyone to find Jesus Christ. After you die, meet Jesus Christ; and, if he brings you back to do something, nothing else will faze you. I have completed what Jesus wants me to do for now. There are other things, but not until this is available to everyone. Now, God will provide the means to publish and market this book. It has been over a five-year journey. Just remember, we are the light in this world. We must continue to spread the gospel of Jesus Christ until we are with him. Your mind cannot comprehend God and how his love for us feels. I can tell you it is worth dying for.

5 and 1/2 years ago I was going to work every day and living mostly an empty life. Now, I will be using all my time and energy for a real purpose. My life now switches to someone who has met his maker, found the narrow path, and now I must protect it. I must fight evil every day. At my disposal is the ultimate weapon, the Word of God. Now Jesus, my king, wants me to fight any evil in my path and I have the power of Jesus Christ behind me. My first mission, getting this book out for everyone, is complete. Now the fun part. Crush evil any way possible. Satan took his best shot; Jesus Christ crushed him and has given me the power to do the same thing.

God Bless, now I pass the torch to you,

Manuel Giorgi

BIBLIOGRAPHY

Baxter, Mary K. *A Divine Revelation of Hell.* New Kensington, PA: Whitaker House, 1997.

Baxter, Mary K., and T.L. Lowery. *A Divine Revelation of Heaven.* New Kensington, PA: Whitaker House, 1998.

Crossway Bibles. *The Holy Bible, English Standard Version.* Wheaton, IL: Crossway Bibles, 2001.

O'Neal, Sam. "When Was the Bible Assembled." Learn Religions, 2019. https://www.learnreligions.com/when-was-the-bible-assembled-363293

Wiese, Bill. *23 Minutes in Hell: One Man's Story about What He Saw, Heard, and Felt in That Place of Torment.* Lake Mary, FL: Charisma House, 2006.

ACKNOWLEDGMENTS

I thank God. During all these trials in my life, God always got me through it. God gave me the time to write this book. Even though it is my second one, this is the complete one. I needed more time, more revelations, and more information from God. So, I thank God for that and my wonderful son. God assured me that my son is blessed, no matter what happens. Lastly, it bothered me that I could not remember everything that happened when I died. Thank you, God, for showing it to me on December 7, 2022. It really was the perfect time.

I want to thank my mother who has seen most of my trials in life. After my father passed away, she wanted me to be there for her. Six months later, she was the one who called for help when I died.

About the author:

Manuel Giorgi

North Providence, RI

manny.giorgi@gmail.com

Facebook: Manuel Giorgi

Author of: "I Died To Meet Jesus"

www.revivedbyjesus.com